Sermons for the Times

Charles Kingsley

Sermons for the Times

ISBN: 979-8-88830-951-3

CONTENTS

SERMON I

'FATHERS AND CHILDREN'

Behold, I will send you Elijah the prophet before the
coming of the great and dreadful day of the Lord:
And he shall turn the heart of the fathers to the
children, and the heart of the children to their fathers,
lest I come and smite the earth with a curse.

Malachi iv. 5, 6.

These words are especially solemn words. They stand in an especially solemn and important part of the Bible. They are the last words of the Old Testament. I cannot but think that it was God's will that they should stand where they are, and nowhere else. Malachi, the prophet who wrote them, did not know perhaps that he was the last of the Old Testament prophets. He did not know that no prophet would arise among the Jews for 400 years, till the time when John the Baptist came preaching repentance. But God knew. And by God's ordinance these words stand at the end of the Old Testament, to make us understand the beginning of the New Testament. For the Old Testament ends by saying that God would send to the Jews Elijah the prophet. And the New Testament begins by telling us of John the Baptist's coming as a prophet, in the spirit and power of Elias; and how the Lord Jesus himself declared plainly that John the Baptist was Elijah who was to come; that is, the Elijah of whom Malachi prophesies in my text.

Therefore, we may be certain that this text tells us what John the Baptist's work was; that John the Baptist came to turn the hearts of the fathers to the children, and the hearts of the children to the fathers; lest the Lord should come and smite the land with a curse.

Some may be ready to answer to this, 'Of course John the Baptist came to warn parents of behaving wrongly to their children, if they were careless or cruel; and children to their parents, if they were disobedient or ungrateful. Of course he would tell bad parents and children to repent, just as he came to tell all other kinds of sinners to repent. But that was only a part of John the Baptist's work. He came to be the forerunner of the Messiah, the Saviour, the Redeemer.'

Be it so, my friends. I only hope that you really do believe that John the Baptist did come to proclaim that a Saviour was born into the world—provided only that you remember all the while who that Saviour was. John the Baptist tells you who He was. If you will only remember that, and get the thought of it into your hearts, you will not be inclined to put any words of your own in place of the prophet Malachi's, or to fancy that you can describe better than Malachi what John the Baptist's work was to be; and that turning the hearts of the fathers to the children, and the hearts of the children to the fathers, was only a small part of John the Baptist's work, instead of being, as Malachi says it was, his principal work, his very work, the work which must be done, lest the Lord, instead of saving the land, should come and smite it with a curse.

Yes—you must remember who it was that John the Baptist came to bear record of, and to manifest or show to the Jews. The Angels on the first Christmas Eve told us—they said it was The Lord, 'Unto you,' they said, 'is born a Saviour, who is Christ, The Lord.'

John the Baptist told you and all mankind who it was—that it was The Lord. 'The voice of one crying in the wilderness, Prepare ye the way of the Lord!'

The Lord. What Lord—Which Lord? John the Baptist knew. Simeon, Anna, Nathaniel, all righteous and faithful hearts who waited for the salvation of the Lord, knew. The Pharisees and Sadducees did not know. The men who wrote our Creeds, our Prayer Book, our Church Catechism, knew. The Pharisees and the Sadducees in our day, who fancy themselves wiser than the Creeds, and the Prayer Book, and the Church Catechism, do not know. May God grant that we may all know, not only with our lips, but with our hearts, our faith, our love, our lives, who The Lord is.

Jesus Christ, the babe of Bethlehem, is The Lord. But who is He? The Bible tells us; when we have heard what the Bible tells us we shall be able better to understand the text. The Lord is He of whom it is written, 'And God said, Let us make man in our image, after our likeness.' And who is God's image and God's likeness? The New Testament tells us—Jesus Christ. In Him man was made. He is the Son of Man, who is in heaven—the true perfect pattern of man: but He is also the image and likeness of God, the brightness of His Father's glory, and the express image of His person. He is The Lord. He is the Lord who instituted marriage, and said, 'It is not good that the man should be alone; I will make him an help-meet for him.' He is the Lord who said to man, 'Be fruitful and multiply: fill the earth and subdue it.' He is the Lord who said to the first murderer, 'Thy brother's blood crieth against thee from the ground.' He is the Lord who talked with Abraham face to face as a man talks with his friend; who blest him by giving him a son in his old age, that he might be the father of many nations. He is the Lord who, on Mount Sinai, gave those Ten Commandments, the foundation of all law and right order between man and God, between man and man:—'Thou shalt honour thy father and thy mother. Thou shalt do no murder. Thou shalt not commit adultery. Thou shalt not steal. Thou shalt not bear false witness in courts of law or elsewhere. Thou shalt not covet thy neighbour's property.'

This is The Lord. Not a God far away from men; who does not feel for them, nor feel with them; not a God who despises men, or has an ill-will to men, and must be won over to change his mind, and have mercy on them, by many supplications and tears, and fear and trembling, and superstitious ceremonies. But this is The Lord, this is the babe of Bethlehem, this is He whose way John the Baptist came to prepare—even He of whom it is written, that He possessed wisdom, the simple, practical human wisdom, useful for this everyday earthly life of ours, which Solomon sets forth in his Proverbs, in the beginning before His works of old; and that when He appointed the foundations of the earth, that Wisdom was by Him, as one brought up with Him, and she was daily His delight; rejoicing alway before Him; rejoicing in the habitable parts of the earth; and her delights were with the sons of men.

In one word, He is the Lord, in whose likeness man is made. Man's justice is a pattern of His; man's love is a pattern of His; man's industry a pattern of His; man's Sabbath-rest, in some unspeakable and eternal way, a pattern of His. Man's family ties are patterns of His. God the Father is He, said St. Paul, from whom every fathership in heaven and earth is named, that we may be such fathers to our children as God is to us. God The Son is He who is not ashamed to call us brethren, and to declare to us the glorious news, that in Him we, too, are the sons of God, that we may be such sons to our heavenly Father—ay, and to our earthly fathers also, as the Lord Jesus was to His Father.

Yes—and even more wonderful still, and more blessed still, the Lord is not ashamed to call himself a husband. Our human wedlock and married love is a pattern of some divine mystery. 'Husbands love your wives, as Christ also loved the Church, and gave Himself for it, that He might present it to Himself a glorious Church, not having spot or wrinkle, but that it should be holy and without blemish.' Blessed words, which we cannot pretend to explain or understand, but can only believe and adore, and find, as we shall find, in proportion as we are loving and faithful in wedlock, that

God's Spirit bears witness with our spirit, that they are reasonable, blessed, true; true for ever.

This, then, was the Lord who was coming to judge these Jews; not merely a god, but The God. The Lord, in whose likeness man was made; who had appointed men to be fathers, sons, husbands, citizens of a nation, owners of property, subject to laws, and yet makers of laws; because all these things, in some wonderful way, are parts of His likeness. He was coming to this nation of the Jews first, and then to all the nations of the earth, to judge them, Malachi said, with a great and terrible day. To lay the axe to the root of the tree; to cut down from the very root the evil principles which were working in society. His fan was in His hand; and He would thoroughly purge His floor; and gather His wheat into the garner, for the use of future generations: but the chaff, all that was empty, light, and useless, He would burn up and destroy utterly out of the way, with unquenchable fire. He would inquire of every man, How have you kept my image; my likeness, in which I made you? What sort of husbands, fathers, sons, neighbours, subjects, and governors, have you been? And above all, Malachi says, the root question of all would be, what sort of fathers have you been to your children? What sort of children to your fathers? Does that seem to you a small question, my friends? Would you have rather expected to hear John the Baptist ask, what sort of saints they had been? What sort of doctrines they were professing?

A small question? Look at these two little words, Father and Son. Father and Son! Are they not the most deep and awful, as well as the most blessed and hopeful words on earth? Do they not tell us the very mystery of God's being? Are they not the very name of God, God The Father and God The Son, knit together by one Holy Spirit of Love to each other and to all, who proceeds alike from The Father and from The Son? And then, will you think it a light matter to ask fallen creatures made in the likeness of that perfect Father and that perfect Son, what sort of fathers and sons they have been? God help us all, and give us grace to ask ourselves that question morning and night, before the great and terrible day of the Lord come, lest He come and smite this land with a curse.

I have been led to think deeply and to speak openly upon this solemn matter, my friends, by seeing, as who can help seeing, the great division and estrangement between the old and the young which is growing up in our days. I do not, alas! I cannot, deny the complaints which old people commonly make. Old people complain that young people are grown too independent, disobedient, saucy, and what not. It is too true, frightfully, miserably true, that there is not the same reverence for parents as there was a generation back;—that the children break loose from their parents, spend their parents' money, choose their own road in life, their own politics, their own religion, alas! too often, for themselves;—that young people now presume to do and say a hundred things which they would not have dreamed in old times. And they are ready enough to cry out that all this is a sign of the last days, of which, they say, St. Paul speaks in 2 Tim. iii. 4—when men 'shall be disobedient to parents, unthankful, boasters, heady, high-minded, despisers of those who are good, lovers of pleasure more than lovers of God.' My friends, my friends, it is far better for us who have children, instead of prying into the times and seasons which God has kept in His own hand, to read our Bibles faithfully, and when we quote a text, quote the whole of it, and not just those bits of it which help us to throw blame on other people. What St. Paul really says, is that 'in the last days evil times will come;' just as they had come, he shows, when he wrote; and what he means I will try and show you presently. And, moreover, remember that Malachi says, that the hearts of the parents in Judea needed turning to their children, as well as the hearts of the children to their parents. Take care lest it be not so in England now.   Remember that St. Paul, in that same solemn passage, gives other marks of 'last days,' which have to do with parents as well as with children, and some which can only have to do with parents—for they are the sins of grown-up and elderly people, and not of young ones. He says, that in those days men shall also be 'covetous, proud, without natural affection, breakers of their word, blasphemers; having a form of godliness, but denying the power thereof.' Will none of these hard words hit some grown people in our day? Will not they fill some of us with dread, lest the parents now-a-days should be as much in fault as the children of whom they complain; lest the parents' sins should be but too often the cause of the children's sins? Read through St. Paul's sad list of sins, and see how every young man's sin in it has some old man's sin corresponding to it. St. Paul does not part his list, and I dare not, and cannot.   St. Paul mixes the parents' and the children's sins together in his words, and I fear that we do the same in our actions.

Oh! beware, beware, you who complain of the behaviour of children now-a-days, lest your children have as much cause to complain of you. Are your children selfish, lovers of themselves?— See that you have not set them the example by your own covetousness or laziness. Are they boastful?—See that your pride has not taught them. Incontinent and profligate?—See that your own fierceness has not taught them. If they see you unable to master your own temper, they will not care to try to master their appetites. Are they disobedient and unthankful?—See, well, then that your want of natural affection to them, your neglect, and harshness, and want of feeling and tenderness, has not made the balance of unkindness fearfully even between you. Are your children disobedient to you?—See that you have not taught them to be so, by breaking your word to them, by letting them see you deceitful to others, till they have lost all trust in you, all reverence for you. Above all, are your children lovers of pleasure more than lovers of God?—Oh! beware, beware, lest you have made them so,—lest you have been blasphemers against God, even when you have been fancying that you talked religion. Beware lest you have been teaching them dark, cruel, superstitious thoughts about God,—making them look up to Him not as their heavenly Father, but as a stern taskmaster whom they must obey, not from gratitude, but from fear of hell, and so have made God look so unlovely in their eyes that 'there is no beauty in Him that they should desire Him.' Can you wonder at their loving pleasure rather than loving God, when you show them nothing in God's character to love, but everything to dread and shrink from? And last of all, are your children despisers of those who are good, inclined to laugh at religion, to suspect and sneer at pious people, and call them hypocrites? Oh! beware, beware, lest your lip-religion, your dead faith, your inconsistent practice, has not been the cause of it. If you, as St. Paul says, have a form of godliness, and yet in your life and actions deny the power of it, by living without God in the world, and following the lowest maxims of the world in everything but what you call the salvation of your souls, what wonder if your children grow up despisers of those who are good? If they see you preaching one thing, and practising another, they will learn to fancy that all godly people do the same. If they see your religion a sham, they will learn to fancy all religion false also. Oh! woe, woe, most terrible, to those who thus harden their own children's hearts, and destroy in them, as too many do, all faith in God and man, all hope, all charity! Woe to them! for the Lord Himself, who came to lay the axe to the root of the tree, said of such, 'If any man cause one of these little ones to offend, it were better for him that a millstone were hanged about his neck, and that he were drowned in the depths of the sea.'

So it is too often now-a-days, and so it will be, until people condescend to learn over again that simple old Church Catechism which they were taught when they were little, and to teach it to their children, not only with their lips but in their lives.

'The Church Catechism!' some here will say to themselves with a smile, 'that is but a paltry medicine for so great a disease—a pitiful ending, forsooth, to such a severe sermon as this, to recommend just the Church Catechism!' Let those laugh who will, my friends. If you think you can bring up your children to be blessings to you,—if you think you can live so as to be blessings to your children, without the Church Catechism, you can but try. I think that you will fail. More and more, year by year, I find that those who try do fail. More and more, year by year, I find that even religious people's education of their children fails, and that pious men's sons now-a-days are becoming more and more apt to be scandals to their parents and to religion. If any choose to say that the reason is, that the pious men's sons were not of the number of the elect, though their fathers were, I can only answer, that God is no respecter of persons, and that they say that He is; that God is not the author of the evil, and that they say that He is. If a child of mine turns out ill, I am bound to lay the fault first on myself, and certainly never on God,—and so is every man, unless the inspired Scripture is wrong where it says, 'Train up a child in the way he should go, and when he is old he will not depart from it.' And the fault is in ourselves. Very few people really teach their children now-a-days the Church Catechism; very few really believe the Church Catechism; very few really believe that God is such an one as the Church Catechism declares to us; very few believe in the Lord, in whose image and likeness man is made, whose way John the Baptist prepared by turning the hearts of the fathers to the children. They put, perhaps, religious books into their children's hands, and talk to them a great deal about their souls: but they do not tell their children what the Church Catechism tells them, because they do not believe what the Church Catechism tells them.

What that is; what the Church Catechism does tell us, which the favourite religious books now-a-days do not tell us; and what that has to do with turning the hearts of the fathers to the children, I must tell you hereafter. God grant that my words may sink into all hearts, as far as they are right and true; if sooner or later we are not all brought to understand the meaning of those two simple words, Father and Son, neither Baptism, nor Confirmation, nor Schools, nor this Church, nor the very body and blood of Him who died for us, to share which you are all called this day, will be of avail for the well-being of this parish, or of this country, or any other country upon earth. For where the root is corrupt, the fruit will be also; and where family life and family ties, which are the root and foundation of society, are out of joint, there the Nation and the Church will decay also; as it is written, 'If the foundations be cast down, what can the righteous do?'

And whensoever, in any family, or nation and church, the root of the tree (which is the conduct of parents to children, and of children to parents) grows corrupt and rotten, then 'last days,' as St.

Paul calls them, are indeed come to it, and evil times therewith; for the Lord will surely lay the axe to the root of it, and cut it down and cast it into the fire: neither will the days of that family, or that people, or that Church, be long in the land which the Lord their God has given them. So it has been as yet, in all ages and in all countries on the face of God's earth, and so it will be until the end. Wheresoever the hearts of the fathers are not turned to the children, and the hearts of the children to the fathers, there will a great and terrible day of the Lord come; and that nation, like Judæa of old, like many a fair country in Europe at this moment, will be smitten with a curse.

SERMON II

SALVATION

This is life eternal, that they may know Thee, the only true God, and Jesus Christ whom Thou hast sent.

John xvii. 3.

Before I can explain what this text has to do with the Church Catechism, I must say to you a little about what it means.

Now if I asked any of you what 'salvation' was, you would probably answer, 'Eternal life.'

And you would answer rightly. That is exactly what salvation is, and neither more nor less. No more than that; for nothing greater than that can belong to any created being. No less than that; for God's love and mercy are eternal and without bound.

But what is eternal life?

Some will answer, 'Going to heaven when we die.' But what before you die? You do not know? cannot tell?

Let us listen to what God Himself says. Let us listen to what the Lord Jesus Christ, the Word of God, says. Let us listen to what He who spake as man never spake, says. Surely His words must be the clearest, the simplest, the most exact, the deepest, the widest; the exactly fit and true words, the complete words, the perfect words, which cannot be improved on by adding to them or taking away one jot or tittle. What did the Lord Jesus Christ say that eternal life was?

'This is eternal life, that they may know Thee the only true God, and Jesus Christ whom Thou hast sent.'

To know God and Jesus Christ; that is eternal life. That is all the eternal life which any of us will ever have, my friends. Unless our Lord's words are not complete and perfect, and do not tell us the truth, the whole truth, and nothing but the truth, about eternal life, that is all the eternal life any one will ever have; and we must make up our minds to be content therewith.

To which some will answer, almost angrily, 'Of course. The way to obtain eternal life is to know God and Jesus Christ; for if we do not, we cannot obtain it.'

What words are these, my friends? what rash words are these, which men thrust into Scripture out of their own carnal conceits, as if they could improve upon the speech of the Son of Man Himself? He says, not that to know God is the way to eternal life: but rather that eternal life is the way to know God. He does not say, This is to know God and Jesus Christ, in order that they may have eternal life. Whatever He says, He does not say that. Nay, more, if we are to be very exact (and can we be too exact?) with the Lord's words, He says, that 'This is eternal life, in order that they may know God and Jesus Christ.' Not that we are to know God that we may obtain eternal life, but that we must have eternal life in order that we may know God; that eternal life is the means, and the knowledge of God the end and purpose for which eternal life is given us. However this may be, at least He says what the noble collect which we repeat every Sunday says, 'That our eternal life stands in the knowledge of God,' depends on it, and will fall without it.

'That we may know God.' Not merely that we may know doctrines about salvation, and the ways of winning God's favour, and turning away His vengeance; not merely to know what God has done ages ago, or may do ages hence, for us: but to know God Himself; to know His person, His likeness, His character; and what He is, and what He does, now and always; to know His righteousness, His goodness, His truth, His love, His mercy, His strength, His willingness and mightiness to save; in a word, what the Bible calls His glory; and therefore to admire and delight in Him utterly. That is what our eternal life stands in; that is why God has given to us eternal life in His Son, that we may know that. Oh, believe your Saviour simply, like little children, and enter into the joy of your Lord. Acquaint yourselves with God, and be at peace.

To know God; and also to know Jesus Christ whom He has sent. For St. John, when he tells us that God has already given to us eternal life, says also, that this life is in His Son. To know the Son of God, in whom the Father is well pleased, because He is His perfect Son; His exact likeness, the likeness of that glory of His, and the express image of that person and character of His, which I described to you just now; One whose life was and is and ever will be eternally all love, and mercy, and self-sacrifice, and labour, for lost and sinful men; all trust and obedience to His Father. To know Him and His life, and to come to Him, and receive from Him an eternal life, which this world did not give us, and cannot take away from us; which neither man, devil, nor angel, nor the death of our bodies, the ruin of empires, the destruction of the whole universe, and of time, and space, and all things whereof man can conceive or dream, can alter in the slightest, because it is a life of goodness, and righteousness, and love, which are eternal as the God from whom they spring; eternal as Christ, who is the same yesterday, to-day, and for ever; and nothing but our own sinful wills can rob us of them.

This is eternal life, and therefore this is salvation. A very different account of it (though it is the Bible account) from that narrow and paltry one which too many have in their minds now-a-days; a narrow and paltry notion that it means only being saved from the punishment of our sins after we die; and a very unbelieving, and godless, and atheistical notion too; which, like all unbelief hurts and spoils men's lives.

For too many say to themselves, 'God must save me after I am dead, of course, for no one else can: but as long as I am alive I must save myself. God must save me from hell; but I must save myself from poverty, from trouble, from what the world may say of me or do to me, if I offend it.' And so salvation seems to have to do altogether with the next life, and not at all with this; and people lose entirely the belief that God is our deliverer, our protector, our guide, our friend, now, here, in this life; and do not really think that they can get on better in this world by knowing God and Jesus Christ; and so they set to work to help themselves by cunning, by covetousness, by cowardly truckling to the wicked ways of the very world which they renounced at baptism, by following after a multitude to do evil, and standing by, saying, 'I saw it not,' when they see wrong and cruelty done upon the earth; afraid to fight God's battles like men of God, because they say it is 'dangerous.' And so, in these evil days, thousands who call themselves Christians live on, worldly and selfish, without God in the world; while they talk busily enough of 'preparing to meet God,' in the world to come; dreaming, poor souls, of arriving at what they call 'salvation' after they die, while they are too often, I fear, deep enough in what the Scripture calls 'damnation,' before they die.

'But,' say some, 'is not salvation going to a place called heaven?' My friends, let the Bible speak. It tells us that salvation is not in a place at all, but in a person, a living, moving, acting person, who is none other than the Lord Jesus Christ. Let the Psalmists speak, and shame us, who ought to know (being Christians) even better than they, that The Lord Himself is Salvation. The whole Book of Psalms, what is it but the blessed discovery that salvation is not merely in a place, or a state, not even in some 'beatific vision' after men die; but in the Lord Himself all day long in this world; that salvation is a life in God and with God? 'The Lord is my light, and my salvation, of whom then shall I be afraid? The Lord is the strength of my life, and my portion for ever.' This is their key-note.

Shame on us Christians, that we should have forgotten it for one so much lower. 'The name of the Lord,' says Solomon, 'is a strong tower: the righteous runneth into it, and is safe.' Into it: not merely into some pleasant place after he dies, but all day long; and is safe: not merely after he dies, but in every chance and change of this mortal life. My friends, I am ashamed to have to put Christian men in mind of these things. Truly, 'Evil communications have corrupted good manners; awake to righteousness and sin not, for some have not the knowledge of God.' I am ashamed, I say; for there are old hymns in the mouths of every one to this day, which testify against their want of faith; which say, 'Christ is my life,' 'Christ is my salvation;' and which were written, I doubt not, by men who meant literally what they said, whatever those who sing them now-a-days may mean by them. Now what do those hymns mean by such words, if they mean anything at all? Surely what I have been preaching to you, and what seems to some of you, I fear, strange and new doctrine. And what else does the Church Catechism mean, when it bids every child thank God for having brought him into a state of salvation? For mind, throughout the whole Church Catechism there is not one word about what people commonly call heaven and hell; not one word though 'heaven and hell' are now-a-days generally the first things about which children are taught. Not one word is the child taught about what will happen to him after death, except that his body will rise again, and that Christ will be his Judge after he is dead as well as while he is alive: but not one word about that salvation after he is dead, which is almost the only thing of which one hears in many pulpits. And why, but because the Catechism teaches the child to believe that Jesus Christ is his salvation now, in this life, and believes that to be enough for him to know? For if Christ be eternal, His salvation must be eternal also. If Christ's life be in the child, eternal life must be in the child; for Christ's life must be eternal, even as Christ Himself; and that is enough for the child, and for us also.

And with this agrees that great text of Scripture, 'When the wicked man turneth away from his wickedness, and doeth that which is lawful and right, he shall save his soul alive.' People now-a-days are apt to make two mistakes about that one text. First they forget the 'when,' and read it as if it stood, 'If the wicked man turn away from his wickedness in this life, he shall save his soul in the next life:' but the Bible says much more than that. It says, that when he turns, then and there, that moment he shall save his soul alive. And next, they read the text as if it stood, 'he shall save his soul.' Here again, my friends, the Bible says a great deal more; it says, that he shall save his soul alive. Perhaps that does not seem to you any great difference? Alas, alas, my friends, I fear that there are too many now, as there have been in all times, who do not care for the difference. Provided 'their souls are saved,' by which they mean, provided they escape torment after they die, it matters nothing to them whether their souls are saved alive, or saved dead; they do not even know the difference between a dead soul and a live soul; because they know nothing about eternal death and eternal life, which are the death and the life of eternal persons such as souls are; they say to themselves, if they be Protestants, 'I hope I shall have faith enough to be saved;' or if they be Papists, 'I hope I shall have good works enough to be saved;' valuing faith and works not for themselves; yea, valuing—for I must say it—Almighty God Himself, not for Himself and His own glory, but valuing faith and works, and the Father, and the Son, and the Holy Spirit, only because, as they dream, they are so many helps to a life of pleasure beyond the grave; not knowing this, that living faith and good works do not merely lead to heaven, but are heaven itself, that true, real eternal heaven wherein alone men really live; that true, real eternal life which was with the Father, and was manifested in Jesus Christ, whom St. John saw living upon earth that same Eternal Life, and bore witness of Him that His life was the light of men; that eternal life whereof it is written, that God hath brought us to life together with Christ, and raised us up, and made us sit together in heavenly places in Christ Jesus:—not knowing this, that the only life which any soul ought to live, is the life of God and of Christ, and of the Spirit of God and Christ; a life of righteousness, and justice, and truth, and obedience, and mercy, and love; a life which God has given to us, that we may know and copy Him, and do His works, and live His life, for ever:— not knowing this also that eternal death is not merely some torture of fire and worms beyond the grave: but that this is eternal death, not to live the eternal life which is the only possible life for souls, the life of righteousness and love; a death which may come on respectable people, and high religious professors, while they are fancying themselves sure to be saved, as easily and surely as it may on thieves and harlots, wallowing in the mire of sins.

For what is this same eternal death? The opposite surely to eternal life. Eternal life is to know God, and therefore to obey Him. Eternal life is to know God, whose name is love; and therefore, to rejoice to fulfil His law, of which it is written, 'Love is the fulfilling of the law;' and therefore to be full of love ourselves, as it is written, 'We know that we have passed from death unto life, because we love the brethren;' and again, 'Every one that loveth, knoweth God, for God is love.' And on the other hand, eternal death is not to know God, and therefore not to care for His law of love, and therefore to be without love; as it is written on the other hand, 'He that loveth not his brother abideth in death.' 'Whosoever hateth his brother is a murderer;' and ye know that no murderer hath eternal life abiding in him; and again, 'He that loveth not, knoweth not God, for God is love.' Eternal death, then, is to love no one; to be shut up in the dark prison-house of our own wilful and wayward thoughts and passions, full of spite, suspicion, envy, fear; in fact, in one word, to be a devil. Oh, my friends, is not that damnation indeed, to be a devil here on earth, and for aught we know, for ever and ever?

Do you not know what frame of mind I mean? Thank God, none of us, I suppose, is ever utterly without some grain of love left for some one; none of us, I suppose, is ever utterly shut up in himself; and as long as there is love there is life and as long as there is life there is hope: but yet there have been moments when one has felt with horror how near, and how terrible, and how easy was this same eternal death which some fancy only possible after they die.

For, my friends, were you ever, any one of you, for one half hour, completely angry, completely sulky? displeased and disgusted with everybody and everything round you, and yet displeased and disgusted with yourself all the while; liking to think everyone wrong, liking to make out that they were unjust to you; feeling quite proud at the notion that you were an injured person: and yet feeling in your heart the very opposite of all these fancies: feeling that you were wrong, that you were unjust to them, and feeling utterly ashamed at the thought that they were the injured persons, and that you had injured them. And perhaps, to make all worse, the person about whom all this storm had arisen in your heart, was some dear friend or relation whom you loved (strange contradiction, yet most true) at the very moment that you were trying to hate. Oh, my friends, if one such dark hour has ever come home to you; if you have ever let the sun go down upon your wrath, and so given place to the devil, then you know something at least of what eternal death is. You know how, in such moments, there is a worm in the heart, and a fire in the heart, compared with which all bodily torment would be light and bearable; a worm in the heart which does not die: and a fire in the heart which you cannot quench: but which if they remained there would surely destroy you. So intolerable are they, that you feel that you will actually and really die, in some strange unspeakable way, if you continue in that temper long. Do not there open at such times within our hearts black depths of evil, a power of becoming wicked, a chance of being swept off into sin if one gives way, which one never suspected till then; and yet with all these, the most dreadful sense of helplessness, of slavery, of despair?—God grant that may not remain, for then comes the mad hope to escape death by death, to try by one desperate stroke to rid oneself of that self which is for the time one's torment, worm, fire, death, and hell. And what is this dark fight within us? What does the Bible call it? It is death and life, eternal death and eternal life, salvation and damnation, hell and heaven, fighting together within our hapless hearts, to see which shall be our masters. It is the battle of the evil spirit, who is the Devil, fighting with the good spirit, who is God. Nothing less than that, my friends. Yes, in those hateful and shameful moments of pride, or spite, or contempt, or self-will, or suspicion, or sneering, on which when they are past we look back with shame and horror, and wonder how we could have been such wretches even for a moment,—at such times, I say, our heart is a battle-field, on which no less than the Devil himself, and God Himself are fighting for our souls. On one side, Satan trying to bring us into that state of eternal death in which he lives himself; Satan, the loveless one, the self-willed one, the accuser, the slanderer, slandering God to us, slandering man to us, slandering to us the friends we love best and trust most utterly; yea, slandering our own selves to us, trying to make us believe that we are as bad, ought to be as bad, and must always be as bad as we seem for the time to be; that we cannot shake off our evil passions, that we cannot rise again out of the eternal death of sin into the eternal life of righteousness. And on the other side, the Spirit of God and of His Christ, the Spirit of eternal life, the Spirit of justice, and righteousness, love, joy, peace, duty, self-sacrifice, trying to make us know Him and see His beauty, and obey Him, and be at peace; trying to raise us again into that eternal life and state of salvation which the Lord Jesus Christ has bought for us with His most precious blood.

Oh, awful thought! Life and death, the Devil himself, and the Lord Jesus Christ Himself, fighting in your heart and in mine, and in the heart of every human being round us! And yet most blessed thought, hopeful, glorious,—full of the promise of eternal victory! For greater is He that is with us, than he that is against us; and He who conquered Satan for Himself, can and will conquer him for us also. No thing can separate us from the love of Christ; no thing, yea no angel, or devil, principality, or power; no thing, but only ourselves, only our own proud and wayward will and determination to the Devil's voice in our hearts, and not the voice of Christ, the Word of Life, who is nigh us, in our hearts, even in our darkest moments, loving us still, pitying us, ready, able and willing to help all who cast themselves on Him, and raise us, there and then, the very moment we cry to Him and renounce the Devil and our own foolish will, out of self-will into God's will, out of darkness into light, out of hatred into love, out of despair into hope, out of doubt into faith, out of tempest into peace, out of the death of sin into the life of righteousness, the life of love and charity, which abideth for ever. Oh, listen not to the lying, slanderous Devil, who tells you that by your own sin you have lost your share in Christ, lost baptismal grace, lost Christ's love—Lost His love? His, who, were you in the very lowest depths of hell, would pity you still? His love, who Himself went down into hell, and preached to the spirits in prison, to show that he did care even for them? Not so: into Him you have been baptized. His cross is on your foreheads, His Father is your Father:—and can a father desert his child, even though he sinned seventy and seven times, if seventy and seven times he turn and repent? Can man weary God? Can the creature conquer and destroy the love of his Creator? Can Christ deny Himself? Not so; whosoever thou art, however sorely tempted, however deeply fallen, however disgusted and terrified at thyself, turn only to that blessed face which wept over Jerusalem, to that great heart which bled for thee upon the cross, and thou shalt find him unchanged, the same yesterday, to-day, and for ever, the Lord of life and love, able and willing to save to the uttermost all who come to God through Him, and the accusing Devil shall turn and flee, and thou shalt know that thy Redeemer liveth still, and in thy flesh thou shalt see the salvation of God, and cry, 'Rejoice not against me, Satan, mine enemy; for when I fall I shall arise.'

SERMON III

A GOOD CONSCIENCE

*The like figure whereunto baptism doth now save us
(not the putting away the filth of the flesh, but the
answer of a good conscience toward God,) by the
resurrection of Jesus Christ.*

1 Peter iii. 21.

These words are very wide words; too wide to please most people. They preach a very free grace; too free to please most people. Such free and full grace, indeed, that some who talk most about free grace, and insist most on man's being saved only by free grace, are the very men who shrink from these words most, and would be more comfortable in their minds, I suspect, if they were not in the Bible at all, because the grace they preach is too free. But so it always has been, and so it is, and so, I suppose, it always will be. Man preaches his notions of God's forgiveness, his notions of what he thinks God ought to do; but when God proclaims His own forgiveness, and tells men what He has actually done, and bids His apostle declare boldly that baptism doth now save us, then man is frightened at the vastness of God's generosity, and thinks God's grace too free, His forgiveness too complete; and considers this text and many another in the Bible as 'dangerous' forsooth, if it is 'preached unreservedly,' and not to be quoted without some words of man's invention tacked to it, to water it down, and narrow it, and take all the strength and life out of it; and if he be asked whether he believes the words of Scripture,—for instance, whether St. Paul spoke truth when he told the heathen Athenians that they and all men were the offspring of God;—or when he told the Romans that as by the offence of one, judgment came on all men to condemnation, even so by the righteousness of One, the free gift came upon all men to justification of life;—or when he told the Corinthians, that as in Adam all die, even so in Christ shall all be made alive;—or whether St. Peter spoke truth when he said, that 'baptism doth also now save us,'—then they answer, that the words are true 'in a sense;' that is, not in their plain sense; true, if they were only true; true, and yet somehow at the same time not true; and not to be preached 'unreservedly:' as if man could be more cautious and correct in his language than the Spirit of God, who inspired the Apostles; as if man could be more careful of God's honour than God is of His own; as if man could hate sin and guard against sin more carefully than God Himself.

Just in the same way do people stumble at certain invaluable words in the Church Catechism, which teach children to thank God for having brought them into that state of salvation. Even very good people, and people who really wish to believe and honour the Church Catechism, and the Sacrament of Baptism, find these words too strong to please them, and say, that of course a child's being in a state of salvation cannot mean that he is saved, but that he may be saved after he dies.

My friends, I never could find that we have a right to take liberties with the Bible and the Prayer Book which we dare not take with any other book, and to put meanings into the words of them which, in the case of any other book, would be contrary to plain grammar and the English tongue, if not to common sense and honesty.

If you say of a man, 'he is in a state of happiness,' you mean, do you not, that he is happy now, not that he may perhaps be happy some day? If you came to me and told me that you were in a state of hunger, you would think it a very strange answer to receive if I say, 'Very well then, if you become hungry, come to me, and I will feed you?' You all know that a man's being in a state of poverty, or of misery, means that he is poor or miserable now, here, at this very time; that if a man is in a state of sickness, he is sick; if he is in a state of health, he is healthy. Then what can a man's being in a state of salvation mean, by all rules of English, but that he is saved? If I were to say to any one of the good people who do not think so, 'My friend, you are in a state of damnation,' he would answer me quickly enough, 'I am not, for I am not damned.' He would agree that a man's being in a state of damnation means that the man is damned; why will he not agree that a man's being in a state of salvation means that he is saved? Because, my friends, God's grace is too full for fallen man's notions; and therefore there is an evil fashion abroad in the world, that where a text speaks of wrath, and misery and punishment, you are to interpret it exactly, and to the very letter: but where it speaks of love, and mercy, and forgiveness, you are to do no such thing, but narrow it, and fence it, and explain it away, for fear you should make sinners too comfortable,—a plan which seems wise enough, but which, like other plans of man's wisdom, has not succeeded too well, to judge by the number of sinners who are already too comfortable though they hear the Bible misused, and God's grace narrowed in this way every Sunday of their lives.

But, my friends, we call ourselves Englishmen and churchmen; let us be honest Englishmen and plain churchmen, and take our Catechism as it stands. For rightly or wrongly, truly or falsely, it does teach every christened child to thank God, not merely that it has some chance of being saved, when it dies, but that it is saved already, now, here on earth.

Whether that is true or false is another question. I believe it to be true. I believe the text to be true; I believe that why people shrink from it is, that they have got into their minds a wrong, unscriptural, superstitious notion of what being saved, and saving one's soul alive, and salvation mean. And I beg all of you who read your Bibles to search the Scriptures from beginning to end, and try to find out what these words mean, and whether the Catechism has not kept close, after all, to the words of Scripture. It will be better for you, my friends; it will be worth your while, to know exactly what being saved means; for to judge by the signs of the times, there are, very probably, days coming in which it will be as needful for you and for your children to save your souls alive lest you die, as ever it was for the Jews in Isaiah's or Jeremiah's time, or for the Romans in St. Paul's time; and that in that day you will find the Catechism wider, and deeper, and sounder than you have ever suspected it to be, and see, I trust, that in these very words it preaches to you, and me, and our children after us, the one true Gospel and good news, which will stand, and grow, and shine brighter and brighter for ever, when all the paltry, narrow, counterfeit gospels which man invents in its place have been burnt up by the unquenchable fire with which the merciful Lord purges the chaff from His floor.

I told you this morning what I believe that salvation was,—to know God, and Jesus Christ, whom He has sent. To know God's likeness, God's character, what God has shown of His own character, what He has done for us. To know His boundless love, and mercy, and knowing that, to trust in Him utterly, and submit to Him utterly, and obey Him utterly, sure that He loves us, that His will to us is goodwill, that His commandments must be life. To know God, and therefore to love Him and to serve Him, that is salvation.

Now what hinders a little child, from the very moment that it can think or speak, from entering into that salvation? Not the child's own heart. There is evil in the child—true. Is there none in you and me? There is a corrupt nature in the child—true. Is there not in you and me? Woe to us if we have not found it out: woe to us if we dare to think that we are in ourselves—or out of ourselves either—one whit better than our own children. What should hinder any child whom you or I ever saw from knowing God, and His Name, the Father, the Son, and the Holy Spirit?

Has he not an earthly father, through whom he may know The Father? Is he not an earthly son; and through that may he not know The Son? Has he not a conscience, a spirit in him which knows good from evil? holiness from wickedness—far more clearly and tenderly than the souls of most grown people do? and can he not, therefore, understand you when you speak of a Holy Spirit, a Spirit which puts good desires into his heart, and can enable him to bring those good desires into practice?

I know one hindrance at least; and that is his parents' sins; when the parents' harshness or neglect tempts the child to fancy that God The Father is such a Father to him as his parents are, and that to be a child of God is to look up to his heavenly Father with dread and suspicion as to a hard taskmaster whose anger has to be turned away, and not with that perfect love, and trust, and respect, and self-sacrifice, with which the Lord Jesus Christ fulfilled His Father's will and proclaimed His Father's glory: or when the parents' unholiness and lip-religion teach the child to fancy that the Holy Spirit means only certain religious fancies and feelings, or the learning by heart of certain words and doctrines, or, worst of all, a spirit of bondage unto fear; instead of knowing Him to be, as He is, the Spirit of righteousness, and love, and joy, and peace, long-suffering, gentleness, goodness, meekness, temperance: or when, again, parents by their own teaching, do despite to the Spirit of Grace in their own child, and destroy their child's good conscience toward God, by telling the child that it does not really love God, when it loves Him, perhaps, far better than they do; by telling the child that its sins have parted it from God, when its sins are light, yea, are as nothing in the balance compared to the sins they themselves commit every day, while they claim for themselves clearer light and knowledge than the child, and thereby condemn themselves rather than the child; when they darken and defile the pure and beautiful trust and admiration for its Heavenly Father, which God's Spirit puts into the child's heart, by telling it that it is doomed to I know-not-what horrible misery and torture when it dies; but that it can escape from that wretched end by thinking certain thoughts, and feeling certain feelings; and so (after stirring up in the child all manner of dreadful doubts of God's love and justice, and perhaps driving it away from religion altogether by making it believe that it has committed sins which it has not committed, and deserves horrible tortures which it has not deserved), do perhaps at last awaken in it a new love for God, but one which is not like that first love, that childlike love; one which, I fear, is hardly a love for God at all, but principally a selfish joy and delight at having escaped from coming torments. This is the reason, my friends; and this hindrance, at least, I know. I will not copy those parents, my friends, and tell them, as they tell their children, that they are bringing on themselves endless torture; but I must tell them, for the Lord Christ has told them, that they are bringing on themselves something—I know not what—of which it is written, that it were better for them that a millstone were hanged about their necks, and that they were drowned in the depth of the sea. Oh, my friends, if I speak sternly, almost bitterly, when I speak of parents' sins, it is because I speak for those who cannot speak for themselves. I plead for Christ's little ones: I plead for the souls and consciences of those little children of whom Christ said, 'Suffer the little children to come unto me;' not that they might become His, but because they were His already; not that they might win His love, but because He loved them from all eternity: not that they might enter into the kingdom of heaven, but, because they were in the kingdom of heaven already; because the kingdom of heaven was made up of such as them, and the angels who ministered unto them always beheld the face of our Father who is in heaven. Yes; I plead for those children, of whom the Lord said, 'Except ye be converted,' that is, utterly turned and changed, 'and become as little children, ye shall in no wise enter into the kingdom of heaven.' Deep and blessed words, which are the root-rule of all true righteousness; which so few really believe at heart, any more than the Pharisees, and Sadducees, and Herodians of old did. Up and down, all over England, I hear men of all denominations saying, not, 'Except we grown people be converted and become as little children;' but, 'except the little children be converted, and become like us, grown people.' God grant that the little children may not become like too many grown people! God grant it, I say. God grant that our children may not become like us! God grant that they may keep through youth and manhood, and through the grave, and through all worlds to come, the tender and childlike heart, which we too often have hardened in ourselves by bigotry and superstition, and dead faith, and lip-worship! And I can have good hope that God will grant it. I can have hope that God will teach our children and our children's children truly to know Him whose name is Love and Righteousness, the Father, the Son, and the Holy Spirit, as long as I see His providence preserving for us this old Church Catechism, to teach our children what we forget to teach them, or what we have not faith enough to teach them.

Yes, I can have hope for England; and hope for those mighty

nations across the seas, whose earthly mother God has ordained that she should be, as long as the Catechism is taught to her children.

For see. This Catechism does not begin with telling children that they are sinners: they will find that out soon enough for themselves, poor little things, from their own wayward and self-willed hearts. Nor by telling them that man is fallen and corrupt: they will find out that also soon enough, from the way in which they see people go on around them. It does not even begin by telling them that they ought to be good, or what goodness and righteousness is; because it takes for granted that they know that already; it takes for granted that The Light who lights every man who comes into the world is in them; even the Lord Jesus Christ Himself, stirring up in their hearts, as He does in the heart of every child, the knowledge of good and the love of good. But it begins at once by teaching the child the name of God. It goes at once to the root of the matter; to the fountain of goodness itself; even to God, the Father of lights. It is so careful of God's honour, so careful that the child should learn from the first to look up to God with love and trust, that it dare not tell the child that God can destroy and punish, before it has told him that God is a Father and a Maker; the Father of spirits, who has made him and all the world. It dare not tell him that mankind is fallen, before it has told him that all the world is redeemed. It dare not talk to him of unholiness, before it has taught him that the Holy Spirit of God is with him, to make him holy. It tells him of a world, a flesh, and a devil: but he has renounced them. He has neither part nor lot in them; and he is not to think of them yet. He is to think of that in which he has part and lot, of which he is an inheritor. He is to know where he is and ought to be, before he knows where he is not and ought not to be: he is to think of the name of God, by which he can trample world, flesh, and devil under foot, if they dare hereafter meddle with his soul. In its God-inspired tenderness and prudence, it dare not darken the heart of one little child, or tempt him to hard thoughts of God, or to cry, 'Why hast thou made me thus?' lest it put a stumbling-block in the way of Christ's little ones, and dishonour the name and glory of God. It tells him of the love, before it tells him of the wrath; of the order, before it tells him of the disorder; of the right, before the wrong; of the health, before the disease; of the freedom, before the bondage; of the truth, before the lies; of the light, before the darkness; in one word, it tells him first of the eternal and good God, who was, and is, and shall be to all eternity, before and above the evil devil. It tells him of the name of God; and tells him that God is with him, and he with God, and bids him believe that, and be saved, from his birth-hour, to endless ages. It does not tell him to pray that he may become God's child; but to pray, because he is God's child already. It does not tell him to love God, in order that he may make God love him; but to love God because God loves him already, and has loved him from all eternity. It does not tell him to obey Jesus Christ, in order that Christ may save him; but to obey Christ because Christ has saved him, and bought him with his own blood. It does not tell him to do good works, in order that God's Spirit may be pleased with him, and come to him, and make him one of the elect; neither does it tell him, that some day or other, if he is converted, and feels certain religious experiences, he will have a right to consider himself one of God's elect: but it tells him to look man and devil in the face, he, the poor little ignorant village child, and say boldly in the name of God, 'I am one of God's elect. The Holy Spirit of God is sanctifying me, and making me holy. God has saved me; and I heartily thank my Heavenly Father, who has called me to this state of salvation.' It tells him to believe that he is safe—safe in the ark of Christ's Church, as Noah was safe in the ark at the deluge; and that the one way to keep himself within that ark is to obey Him to whom it belongs, who judges it and will guide it for ever, Jesus Christ, the likeness of God; and that as long as he does that, neither world, flesh, nor devil, can harm him; even as Noah was safe in the ark, and nothing could drown him but his own wilful casting himself out of the ark, and trying to free the flood of waters by his own strength and cunning.

It tells him, I say, that he is safe, and saved, even as David, and Isaiah, and all holy men who ever lived have been, as long as he trusts in God, and clings to God, and obeys God; and that only when he forsakes God, and follows his own selfishness and pride, can anything or being in earth or hell harm him.

And do not fancy, my friends, that this is a mere unimportant question of words and doctrines, because a baptized and educated child may be lost after all, and fall from his state of salvation into a state of damnation. Still more, do not fancy that if a child is taught that he is already a child of God, regenerated in baptism, and elect by God's Spirit, that therefore he will neglect either vital faith or good works—heaven forbid!

Is it likely to make a child careless, and inclined to neglect vital truth, to tell him that God is his Father and loves him utterly, and has given His only begotten Son to die for him? Is it not the very way, the only way, to stir up in him faith, and real hearty trust and affection towards God? How can you teach him to trust God, but by telling him that God has shown himself boundlessly and perfectly worthy to be trusted by every soul of man; or to love God, but by showing him that God loves him already? Is it likely to make a child careless of good works, to tell him that God has elected and chosen him, and all his brothers and schoolfellows, to be conformed into the likeness of Jesus Christ, and that every good, and honourable, and gentle thought or feeling which ever crosses his little heart, does not come from himself, is not part of his own nature or character, but is nothing less than the inspiration of the Holy Spirit, nothing less than the voice of Almighty God Himself, speaking to the child's heart, that he may answer with Samuel—'Speak, Lord, for thy servant heareth?' Is it likely to make a child careless about losing eternal life, to tell him that God has already given to him eternal life, and that that life is in His Son Jesus Christ, to whom the child belongs, body, soul, and spirit?

Judge for yourselves, my friends. Think what awe, what reverence, purity, dread of sin, would grow up in a child who was really taught all this, and yet what faith and love to God, what freedom, and joyfulness, and good courage about his own duty and calling in life.

And then look at the fruits which in general follow a religious education, as it is miscalled; and take warning. For if you really train up your children in the way in which they should go, be sure that when they are old they will not depart from it—a promise which is not fulfilled to most religious education which we see around us now-a-days; from which sad fact, if Scripture be inspired and infallible, we can only judge that such is not the way in which the children should go; and that because it is a wrong way, therefore God will not, and man cannot, keep them in it.

SERMON IV

NAMES

And thou shall call his name Jesus.

Matthew i. 21.

Did it ever seem to you a curious thing that the Catechism begins by asking the child its name? 'What is your name?' 'Who gave you this name?' I think that if you were not all of you accustomed to the Church Catechism from your childhood, that would seem a strange way of beginning to teach a child about religion.

But the more I consider, the more sure I am that it is the right way to begin teaching a child what the Catechism wishes to teach.

Do not fancy that it begins by asking the child's name just because it must begin somehow, and then go on to religion afterwards. Do not fancy that it merely supposes that the clergyman does not know the child's name, and must ask it; for this Catechism is intended to be taught by parents to their children, and masters to their apprentices and servants; by people, therefore, who know the child's name perfectly well already, and yet they are to begin by asking the child his name.

Now, why is this? What has a child's name to do with his Faith and duty as a Christian?

You may answer, Because his Christian name is given him when he is baptized.

But why is his Christian name given him when he is baptized? Why then rather than at any other time?

Because it is the old custom of the Church. No doubt it is: and a most wise and blessed custom it is; and one which shows us how much more about God and man the churchmen in old times knew, than most of our religious teachers now-a-days. But how did that old custom arise? What put into the minds of church people, for the last sixteen hundred years at least, that being baptized and being named had anything to do with each other? Men had names of their own long before the Lord Jesus came, long before His Baptism was heard of on earth;—the heathens of old had their names—the heathens have names still;—why, then, did church people feel it

25

right to mix a new thing like baptism with a world-old thing like giving a name?

My friends, I feel and say honestly, that there is more in this matter than I understand; and what little I do understand, I could not explain fully in one sermon, or in many either. But let this be enough for to-day. God grant that I may be able to make you understand me.

Any one's having a name—a name of his own, a Christian name, as we rightly call it—signifies that he is a person; that is, that he has a character of his own, and a responsibility, and a calling and duty of his own, given him by God; in one word, that he has an immortal soul in him, for which he, and he alone, must answer, and receive the rewards of the deeds which it does in the body, whether they be good or evil. But names are not given at random, without cause or meaning. When Adam named all the beasts, we read that whatsoever he called any beast, that was the name of it. The names which he gave described each beast, were taken from something in its appearance, or its ways and habits, and so each was its right name, the name which expressed its nature. And so now, when learned men discover animals or plants in foreign countries, they do not give them names at random, but take care to invent names for them which may describe their natures, and make people understand what they are like, as Adam did for the beasts of old. And much more, in old times, had the names of men each of them a meaning. If it was reasonable to give names full of meaning to each kind of dumb animal, which are mere things, and not persons at all, how much more to each man separately, for each man is a person of himself; each man has a character different from all others, a calling different from all others, and therefore he ought to have his own name separate from all others: and therefore in old times it was the custom to give each child a separate name, which had a meaning in it, was, as it were, a description of the child, or of something particular about the child.

Now, we may see this, above all, in The adorable Name of Jesus. That name, above all others, ought to show us what a name means; for it is the name of the Son of Man, the one perfect and sinless man, the pattern of all men; and therefore it must be a perfect name, and a pattern for all names; and it was given to the Lord not by man, but by God; not after He was born, but before He was conceived in the womb of the blessed Virgin. And therefore, it must show and mean not merely some outward accident about Him, something which He seemed to be, or looked like, in men's eyes: no, the Name of Jesus must mean what the Lord was in the sight of His Father in Heaven; what He was in the eternal purpose of God the

Father; what He was, really and absolutely, in Himself; it must mean and declare the very substance of His being. And so, indeed, it does; for The adorable Name of Jesus means nothing else but God the Saviour—God who saves. This is His name, and was, and ever will be. This Name He fulfilled on earth, and proved it to be His character, His exact description, His very Name, in short, which made Him different from all other beings in heaven or earth, create or uncreate; and therefore, He bears His name to all eternity, for a mark of what He has been, and is, and will be for ever—God the Saviour; and this is the perfect name, the pattern of all other names of men.

Now though the Christian names which we give our children here in England, have no especial meaning to them, and have nothing to do with what we expect or wish the children to be when they grow up, yet the names of people in most other countries in the world have. The Jewish names which we find in the Bible have almost all of them a meaning. So Simeon, I believe, means 'Obedient'; Jehoshaphat means, 'The Lord will judge'; Daniel, 'God is my judge'; Isaiah means, 'The Salvation of the Lord'; Isaac means, 'She laughs,' as a memorial of Sarah's laughing, when she heard that she was to have a child; Ishmael means, 'The Lord hears,' in remembrance of God's hearing Hagar's cry in the wilderness, when Ishmael was dying of thirst.

Especially those names of which we read that God commanded them to be given, have meanings, and to tell the persons who bore those names what God expected of them, or would do for them. So Abraham means, 'The father of many nations.' So the children of both Isaiah and Hosea had names given them by God, each of them meaning something which God was going to do to the nation of the Jews. And so John means, 'Given by the Lord,' which name was given to John the Baptist by the Angel, before his strange birth, in his mother's old age.

But we must remember that the heathens also gave names to their children, though they did not know that their children owed any duty to God, or belonged to God, and therefore we cannot call their names Christian names. Yes, the heathens did give their children names; some of them give their children names still. And there is to me something most sad and painful in those heathen names, and yet most full of meaning. A solemn lesson to us, to show us what the fall means; what man becomes, when he gives way to his fallen nature, and is parted from Christ, the Head of man.

First, these heathens had a dim remembrance that man was made in the likeness of God, and lived by Faith in God, and therefore that men's names were to express that, as indeed many of their old names do. But, alas! the likeness of God in fallen man is like a tree without roots, or rather a tree without soil to grow in. God's likeness in man can only flourish as long as he is joined to Christ, the perfect likeness of God, the true life and the true light of men, the foundation which is already laid, and the soil in which man was meant to grow and flourish for ever, and as long as he is fed by the Spirit of God, the Lord and Giver of Life, who proceeds—never forget that, or you will lose the understanding both of who God is and what man is—proceeds not only from God the Father, but also from God the Son, the Lord Jesus Christ. And therefore, in the heathen, God's likeness withered and decayed, as a tree withers and decays when torn up from the soil. And first, they began to call themselves after the names of false gods, which they had invented out of their own carnal fancies. Then they called themselves after the names of their dumb animal's. So, Pharaoh means, 'The Sun-God'; the Ammonites mean, 'The people who worshipped the ram as a god'; Potiphar means, 'A fat bull,' which the Egyptians used to worship; and I could tell you of hundreds of heathen names more, like these, which are ridiculous enough to make one smile, if we did not keep in mind what tokens they are of sin and ignorance, and the likeness not of God, but of the beasts which perish.

Then comes another set of names, showing a lower fall still, when heathens have quite forgotten that man was originally made in God's likeness, and are not only content to live after the likeness of the beasts which perish, but pride themselves on being like beasts, and therefore name their children after dumb animals,—the girls after the gentler and fairer animals, and the boys after ravenous and cruel beasts of prey. That has been the custom among many heathen nations; perhaps among almost all of them, at some time or other. It is the custom now among the Red Indians in North America, where you will find one man in a tribe called 'The Bull,' another 'The Panther,' and another 'The Serpent,' and so on; showing that they would like to be, if they could, as strong as the bull, as cruel as the panther, as venomous as the serpent. What wonder that those Red Indians, who have so put on the likeness of the beasts, are now dying off the face of the earth like the beasts whom they admire and imitate?

And this was the way with our own heathen forefathers before the blessed Gospel was preached to them. It is frightful, in reading old histories, to find how many Englishmen, our own forefathers, were named after fierce wild beasts, and tried, alas! to be like their names—children of wrath, whose feet were swift to shed blood, under whose lips was the poison of adders, and destruction and bloodshed following in their paths, not knowing the way of peace.

The wolf was the common wild beast of England then; and there are, I should say, twenty common old English names ending in wolf, besides as many more ending in bear, and eagle, and raven. Fearful sign! that men of our own flesh and blood should have gloried in being like the wolf, the cruellest, the greediest, the most mean of savage beasts! How shall we thank God enough, who sent to them the knowledge of His Son Jesus Christ, and called them to be new men in Christ Jesus, and called them to holy baptism, to receive new names, and begin new lives in the righteous likeness of God Himself?—that as by nature they had been the children of wrath, so in baptism they might become the children of grace; that as from their forefathers they had inherited a corrupt nature, original sin, and the likeness of the foul and ravenous beasts which perish, they might have power from the Spirit of God to become the sons of God, conformed into the likeness of Jesus Christ, in peace, and love, and righteousness, and all holiness.

And yet, in names there is a lower depth still among fallen and heathen men; when they lose utterly the last dim notion that God intends men to be persons, even as God the Father is a person, and God the Son a person, and God the Holy Spirit is a person, and so lose the custom of giving their children personal names at all; either giving them, after they grow up, mere nicknames, taken from some peculiarity of their bodies, or something which they have done, or some place where they happen to live; or else, like many tribes of heathen negroes, just name them after the day of the week on which they were born, as some way of knowing them apart; or, last and most shocking of all, give them no names at all, and have no names themselves, knowing each other apart as the dumb animals do, only by sight. I can conceive no deeper fall into utter brutishness than that; and yet some few of the most savage tribes, both in Africa and in the Indian islands, are said—God help them!—to live in that way, and to have no names;—blotted, indeed, out of the book of life!

But is this the right state for men? No; it is the wrong state. It is a disease into which men are fallen; a disease out of which Christ came to raise men; and out of which He does raise us in Holy Baptism. Baptism puts the child into its right state—into the right state for a human being, a human soul, a human person. And baptism declares what that right state is—a member of Christ, a child of God, and an inheritor of the kingdom of heaven. A member of Christ, and therefore a person, because Christ is a person. A child of God, and therefore a person, because a child's duty is to love and trust and obey his father—and only a person can do that, not an animal or a thing. An inheritor of the kingdom of heaven, and therefore bound to cherish all heavenly thoughts and feelings, all righteousness, love, and obedience, which only spirits and persons, not animals or things, can feel.

Now can you not see why baptism is the proper time for giving the child a name? Because then Christ claims the child for His own;—because having a name shows that the child is a person who has a soul, a will, a conscience, a duty; a person who must answer himself for himself alone for what he does in the body, whether it be good or evil. And that will, and soul, and conscience were given the child by Christ, by whom all things are made, who is the Light which lights every man who comes into the world.

Thus in holy baptism God adopts the child for His own in Jesus Christ. He declares that the child is regenerate, and has a new life, a life from above, a seed of eternal personal life which he himself has not by nature. And that seed of eternal life is none other but the Holy Spirit of God, the Spirit of the Father and of the Son, the Lord and Giver of Life, who does verily and indeed regenerate the child in holy baptism, and dwells with his soul, his person, his very self, that He may educate the child's character, and raise his affections, and subdue his will, and raise him up daily from the death of sin to the life of righteousness.

Therefore, when in the Catechism you solemnly ask the child its name, you ask it no light question. You speak as a spirit, a person, to its spirit, to its very self, which God wills should never perish, but live for ever. You single the child out from all its schoolfellows, from all the millions of human beings who have ever lived, or ever will live; and you make the child, by answering to his name, confess that he is a person, an immortal soul, who must stand alone before the judgment seat of God; a person who has a duty and a calling upon God's earth, which he must fulfil or pay the forfeit. And then you ask the child who gave him his name, and make him declare that his name was given him in baptism, wherein he was made a member of Christ and a child of God. You make the child confess that he is a person in Jesus Christ, that Christ has redeemed him, his very self, and taken him to Himself, and made him not merely God's creature, or God's slave, but God's child. You make the child confess that his duty as a person is not towards himself, to do what he likes, and follow his own carnal lusts; but toward God and toward his neighbours, who are in God's kingdom of heaven as well as he. And then you go on in the rest of the Catechism to teach him how he himself, the person to whom you are speaking, may live for ever and ever as a person, by faith in other Persons beside himself, even in God the Father, Son, and Holy Spirit, as you teach him in the Creed; by doing his duty to other persons beside himself, even to God and man, as you teach him in the Ten Commandments; and by diligent prayer to another Person beside himself, even to God his heavenly Father, to feed and strengthen him day by day with that eternal life which was given to him in baptism. Thus the whole Catechism turns upon the very first question in it—'What is thy name?' It explains to the child what is really meant, in the sight of God, and of the Lord Jesus Christ, and of the whole Church in earth and heaven, by the child's having a name of his own, and being a person, and having that name given to him in holy baptism.

And if this is true of our children, my friends, it is equally true of us. You and I are persons, and persons in Christ; each stands alone day and night before the judgment-seat of Christ. Each must answer for himself. None can deliver his brother, nor make agreement unto God for him. Each of us has his calling from his heavenly Father; his duty to do which none can do instead of him. Each has his own sins, his own temptations, his own sorrows, which he must bring single-handed and alone to God his Father, as it is written, 'The heart knoweth its own bitterness, and a stranger intermeddleth not with its joy.' There is a world, a flesh, and a devil, near to us, ready to drag us down, and destroy our personal and spiritual life, which God has given us in Christ; a flesh which tempts us to follow our own appetites and passions, blindly and lawlessly, like the beasts which perish; a world which tempts us to become mere things, without free-wills of our own, or consciences of our own, without personal faith and personal holiness; the puppets of the circumstances and the customs which happen to be round us; blown about like the dead leaf, and swept helplessly down the stream of time. And there is a devil, too, near us, tempting us to the deepest lie of all,—to set up ourselves apart from God, and to try, as the devil tries, to be persons in our own strength, each doing what he chooses, each being his own law, and his own master; that is, his own lawlessness, and his own tyrant: and if we listen to that devil, that spirit of lawlessness and self-will, we shall become his slaves, persons in him, doing his work, and finding torment and misery and slavery in it. Awful thought, that so many enemies should be against us; yea, that we ourselves should be our own enemies! But here baptism gives us hope, baptism gives us courage; we are in Christ; God is our Father, and He can and will give us power to have victory, and to triumph against the world, the flesh, and the devil. His Spirit is given to us in baptism—that Spirit of God who is not merely a force or an influence, but a person, a living, loving, holy Person. He is with us, to give our persons, our souls, eternal life from His life, eternal holiness from His holiness; that so, not merely some part of us, but we our very selves and souls—we the very same persons who were christened, and had a name given us in holy baptism, and have been answering to that name all our life, and were reminded, whenever we heard that name, that we had a duty of our own, a history of our own, hopes, fears, joys, sorrows of our own, which none could share with us,—that we, I say, our own persons, our very selves, may be raised up again at the last day, free, pure, strong, filled with the life of God, which is eternal life.

And then, what blessed words are these from the Lord Jesus, which we read in the book of Revelation? 'And I will give to him that overcometh, a new name.' A new name for him that overcometh world, flesh, and devil; that shall be our portion in the world to come. A new name, perfect like the name of the Lord Jesus, which shall express and mean all that we are to do hereafter, and all that we have done well on earth. A name which shall declare to us our calling and work in God's Church triumphant, throughout all ages and worlds to come: and yet a name which no man knoweth saving he who receiveth it. Yes, if we may dare to guess at the meaning of those deep words, perhaps in that new name shall be recorded for each man all that went on, in the secret depths of the man's own heart, between himself and his God, unknown and unnoticed even by the wife of his bosom. The cup of cold water given in Christ's name; the little private acts of love, and kindness, and self-sacrifice, of which none but God knew; the secret prayers, the secret acts of contrition, the secret hungerings and thirstings after righteousness, the secret struggles and agonies of heart, which he could not, dare not, ought not to tell to any human being. All these, he shall find, will go to make up his character in the life to come, to determine what work he is to do for God in the world to come; as it is written, 'Be thou faithful over a few things, and I will make thee ruler over many things.' All these, perhaps, shall be expressed and declared in that new name, the full meaning of which none will know but the man himself, because none but he knows the secret experiences and struggles which went toward the making of it; none but he and God; for God will know all, He who is the Lord and Saviour of our souls, our persons, our very selves, and can preserve them utterly to the fulness of eternal life, because He knows them thoroughly and utterly; because He judges not according to appearance, but judges righteous judgment; because He sees us not merely as we seem to others to be, not even as we seem at times to ourselves to be;—but searches the heart, and can be touched with the feeling of its infirmities, seeing that He himself has been tempted even as we are, yet without sin; because, blessed thought! He can pierce through the very marrow of our being, and discern the thoughts and intents of our hearts, and see what we long to be, and what we ought to be; so that we can safely and hopefully commend our spirits to His hand, day by day and hour by hour, and can trust Him to cleanse us from our secret faults, and to renew and strengthen our very selves day by day with that eternal life which He gives to all who cast themselves utterly upon Him.

<h1 style="text-align:center">SERMON V</h1>

<h1 style="text-align:center">SPONSORSHIP</h1>

*Whether one member suffer, all the members suffer
with it; or whether one member be honoured, all the
members rejoice with it. Now ye are the body of
Christ, and members in particular.*

1 Cor. xii. 26, 27.

I have to tell you that there will be a confirmation held at ... on the ... All persons of fit age who have not yet been confirmed ought to be ready, and I hope and trust that most of them will be ready, on that day to profess publicly their faith and loyalty to the Lord who died for them. I hope and trust that they will, as soon as possible, tell me that they intend to do so, and come to me to talk over the matter, and to learn what I can teach them about it. They will find in me, I hope, nothing but kindness and fellow-feeling.

But I have not only to tell young persons of the Confirmation: I have to tell all godfathers and godmothers of it also. Have any of you here ever stood godfather or godmother to any young person in this parish who is not yet confirmed? If you have, now is the time for you to fulfil your parts as sponsors. You must help me, and help the children's parents, in bringing your godchildren to confirmation. It really is your duty. It will be better for you if you fulfil it. Better for you, not merely by preventing a punishment, but by bringing a blessing. Let me try to show you what I mean.

Now godparents must have some duty, some responsibility or other;—that is plain. If you or I promise and vow things in another person's name, we must be bound more or less to see that that other person fulfils the promise which we made for him: and so the baptism service warns the sponsors as soon as the child is christened, 'Forasmuch as this child has promised,' &c.; and then we have a plain explanation of what a godfather and godmother's duties are. 'And that your godchild may know these things the better,' &c.: and finally, 'you shall take care that this child be brought to the bishop to be confirmed.'

That is the duty of godfathers and godmothers. Those who stand for any child do it on that understanding, and take upon themselves knowingly that duty.

34

Now, I will not threaten you, my friends; I will not pretend to tell you how God will punish those godfathers and godmothers who do not do their duty; because I do not know how he will punish them. He has not told us in the Bible; and who am I, to deal out God's thunders as if they belonged to me, and judge people of whose real merits and demerits in God's sight I have no fair means of judging? I always dread and dislike threatening any sinner out of this pulpit, except those who plainly break the plain laws which are written in those Ten Commandments, and hypocrites: because I stand in awe of our Lord's own words—'Woe unto you Scribes and Pharisees, hypocrites, for ye bind heavy burdens, and grievous to be borne, and lay them on men's shoulders, while you yourselves touch them not with one of your fingers.' There is too much of that now-a-days, my friends, and I have no mind to add my share to it. And sure I am, that any godfathers and godmothers who do their duty, only because they are afraid that God will punish them if they do not, will not do their duty at all. But sure I am also, and thankful to God, that we cannot neglect any duty whatsoever without being punished in some way or other for our neglect of it. That is not a curse, but a blessing: it is a blessing to us to be punished. The only real curse of God in this life is to be left unpunished for our sins. It is a blessing for us that our sins find us out. For if our sins did not find us out, we should very often, I fear, not find our sins out. And, therefore, when I tell godfathers and godmothers, not that God will perhaps punish them for their neglect, but that He does punish them for it already, I am telling them good news, if they will only open their hearts to that good news.

For God does punish people for neglecting their godchildren. Those who have eyes to see may see it round us now, in this very parish, and in every parish in England, in the selfishness, distrust, divisions, and quarrels which prevail. I do not mean that this parish is worse than others, or England worse than other countries. That is no concern of ours: our own parish, and our own evils, are quite concern enough for us.

Are people happy together? Do they pull well together? Look at the old-standing quarrels, misunderstandings, grudges, prejudices, suspicions, which part one man from another, one family from another; every man for his own house, and very few for the kingdom of God;—no, not even for the general welfare of the parish! Do not men try to better themselves at the expense of the parish—to the injury of the parish? Do not men, when they try to raise their own family, seem to think that the simplest way to do it is to pull down their neighbour's family; to draw away their custom; oust them from their places, or hurt their characters in order to rise upon their fall? so that though they are brothers, members of the same church, nation and parish, the greater part of them are, in practice, at war with each other—trying to live at each other's expense. Now, is this profitable? So far from it, that if you will watch the history, either of the whole world, or of this country, or of this one parish, you will find that by far the greater part of the misery in it has sprung from this very selfishness and separateness—from the perpetual struggle between man and man, and between family and family: so that there have been men, and those learned, and thoughtful, and well-meaning men enough, who have said that the only cure for the world's quarrelling and selfishness was to take all children away from their parents, and bring them up in large public schools; ay, and even to try plans which are sinful, foul, and wicked, all in order to prevent parents knowing which were their own children, that they might care for all the children in the parish as much as if they were their own.

A foolish plan, my friends, and for this one reason, that it is driving out one evil by a still greater one. It destroys the root to get the fruit; by destroying family life, and love, and obedience, to get at the communion of saints, or rather at some ghost of it. The real communion of saints is founded on the Fifth Commandment—'Thou shalt honour thy father and thy mother;' and grows out of it, not by destroying it, but by fulfilling it, as the tree grows out of the root, without taking away from the life of the root, but rather by nourishing and increasing it. Now, the ancient institution of godfathers and godmothers would, it seems to me, if it were carried out honestly and really, do for us what we certainly have not done for ourselves as yet, and bind us all together as one family. It would do all the good which those fanciful philosophers of whom I first spoke, have dreamt, without any of the evil; and it would do it because it goes simply on the belief that the foundation is already laid, and that that foundation is Christ. It says, because this child is not merely the child of his father and mother, but the child of God, the universal Father, therefore other people besides his parents have an interest in him: all who are children of God as well as he have an interest in him; for they are all his brothers, and have a brother's interest in his welfare. Because this child is not merely a member of the family whose surname he bears, but a member of Christ, a member of God's great adopted family, in the hearts of every one of whom His only begotten Son, Jesus Christ, is working; therefore this child ought to be an object of awe, and of interest, and love, and care to every other member of Christ's Church. Moreover, the child is an inheritor of a heavenly kingdom—a kingdom of grace—a kingdom of God,—which is love and justice, and peace, and joy in the Holy Spirit—all personal, spiritual, heavenly, God-given graces;—and he cannot have them without being a blessing to all around him; and he cannot be without them, without being a curse to all around him. If, in after life, when he comes to be confirmed, he claims his inheritance in this heavenly kingdom, he will be full of love, justice, peace, joy in the Holy Spirit. If he refuses to claim his inheritance, and despises his heavenly birthright, and lives as if he were a mere earthly creature, only to please himself, and help himself, he will not be full of those graces. And what then? That he will be full of their opposites, of course. If he has not love, he will be unloving, selfish, hard, cold—to you and yours. If he has not justice he will be unjust—to you and yours. If he is not at peace he will be at war, quarrelling, grudging, envying, backbiting—you and yours. If he has not joy in the Holy Spirit, he will have joy in an unholy spirit, for he must have joy in some spirit; he must take pleasure in some sort of way of thinking and feeling, and some sort of life—in short, in some sort of spirit; and whatsoever is not holy is unholy, whatsoever is not good is bad, whatsoever is not of God's Holy Spirit is of the Devil;—and therefore, if the child as he grows up has not joy in the Holy Spirit, and does not enjoy doing right and pleasing God, and being like the Lord Jesus Christ, then he will enjoy doing wrong, and pleasing himself, and being unlike the Lord Jesus Christ; and so he will set a bad example, and be a temptation to all young people of his own age, ready to lead them into sin, and draw them away to those sinful and unholy pleasures in which he takes delight,—whether it be to rioting and drinking, or to uncleanness and unchastity, or to sneering and laughing at godliness, and at good people. And that, as you know by experience, may be the worse for you and the worse for your children. Is that the sort of young person with whom you would wish to see your children keeping company? Is that the sort of young person next door to whom you would wish to live? Is not such a person a curse, just because he is a person, a spiritual being with an evil spirit in him, which can harm you, and tempt you, and act on you for evil; just as if he had been a righteous person, with the holy and good Spirit in him, he would have helped you, and taught you, and worked on you for good? But so it is: we are members one of another, and if one member goes wrong, and gets diseased, and suffers, all the other members are sure to suffer more or less with it, sooner or later: you feel it so in your bodies—be sure it is so in God's church. But if one member is sound and healthy, all the other members must and will be the better for its health, and rejoice with it, and be able to do their own work the more freely, and strongly, and heartily.

Just think for yourselves; consider, you who are grown up, and have had experience of life, the harm you have known one bad man do, the sorrow he will cause, even to people who never saw him; and the good which you have seen one good man, not merely do with his own hands, but put into other people's hearts by his example. Is not both the good and the harm which is done on earth like the ripple of a stone dropt into water, which spreads and spreads for a vast distance round, however small the stone may be? Indeed, bold as it may seem to say it, I believe that, if we could behold all hearts as the Lord Jesus does, we should find that there never was a good man but that the whole of Christendom, perhaps all mankind, was sooner or later, more or less, the better for him; and that there never was a bad man but that all Christendom, perhaps all mankind, was the worse for him. So fully and really true it is in everyday practice, that we are members one of another.

Now this is the principle on which the Church acts. For the little unconscious infant is treated as what it is, a most solemn and important person, who has other relations beside its father and mother, as a person who is the brother of all the people round it, and of all the Church of God, and who, too, may hereafter do to them boundless good or harm, and they to it.

Therefore we must have some persons to bear witness of that, to remind the child himself, and the whole Church, that he is not merely a soul by itself to be saved, but that he is a brother, a member of a family; that he is bound to that family henceforth, for good and for evil. And this the godfathers and godmothers do: they represent and stand in the place of the whole Church. In one sense, every Christian who meets that child through life, or hears of it, ought to behave, as far as he can, as its godfather; ought to help and improve it if he can. But what is everybody's business, says the proverb, is nobody's business; and therefore these godfathers and godmothers are called out from the rest, as examples to the rest, to watch over the child, and to help and advise its father and mother in guiding and training it: but not by interfering with a parent's rights, God forbid! or by drawing away the child's affections from its own flesh and blood; for if a child be not taught first to honour its father and mother, there is little use in teaching it anything else whatsoever; and a godfather's first duty is to see that his godchild obeys its earthly parents for the Lord's sake, for that is right, and God's will, whatever else is not.

Now just conceive—I am sure that you easily may—what a blessing to this parish, or this part of the country, it would be, were the duties of godfathers really carried out and practised. Every child, beside his father and mother, would have some two or three elder friends at least, whom he had known from his childhood, whom he could trust, to whom he could go in trouble as to his own flesh and blood. The orphan would have, if not relations, still godparents, to comfort and protect him. No one could go abroad without meeting, if not a godparent, yet the godparent or godchild of a friend or a relation; someone, in short, who had an interest in him, and he in them. All would be bound together in threefold cords of interest and affection. How many spites, family quarrels, mistakes, and ignorances about each other would be done away, if people would but thus simply enter into that communion of saints to which, by right, they belong, and bear each other's burdens, and so fulfil the law of Christ.—Unless you think that men are such ill-conditioned creatures that the less they mix with each other the better. I do not. I believe that the more we mix with each other, and the better we know each other, the more we shall feel for each other: that the more we help people, the more we shall find that they are worth helping; that the more, in a word, we try to live, not after the likeness of the beasts, selfish and apart, but after the order and constitution of God's Church, to which we belong, and which is, that we are all fellow-members of one body, then the more we shall find that God's order is the right, good, blessed order, by obeying which we enter into comfort of which we never dream as long as we lead selfish, separate, worldly lives; as it is written, 'Eye hath not seen, nor ear heard, nor hath it entered into the heart of man to conceive, the things which God has prepared for those who love Him.'

This may seem a fanciful dream, too fair to be possible; but what prevents it from being possible, save and except our own selfishness and laziness?

And as for what fruit will spring from it, I have seen, by experience, the blessing of godfathership and godmothership, where it is really carried out; how it will knit together, in sacred bonds of friendship, not merely the children, but the grown persons of different families, and give them a fellow-feeling, a mutual interest, which will prevent a hundred quarrels and coldnesses among frail human creatures. And to those who are childless themselves, what a blessing to have their love and self-sacrifice called out, by being bound in holy bonds, if not to children of their own, at least to children of God!—to have young people to care for, to teach, to guide, and so to win for themselves in the Church of God a name better than that of sons and daughters. And have no fear that by bringing your kindness to bear especially upon your godchildren you will narrow your love, and care less for children in general. Not so, my friends; you will find that your love to your godchildren, like love to your own children, will make all children lovable in your eyes: you will learn how worthy of your love children are, what capacities of good there are in them, how truly of such are the kingdom of heaven; and their simplicity will often teach you more than you can teach them. Their God-given instincts of right and wrong, truth and falsehood, which come from the indwelling Word of God, Jesus the Lord, will often enough shame us, will teach us more and more the depth of that great saying, 'Out of the mouths of babes and sucklings, Thou, O God, hast perfected Thy praise.'

Now try, I entreat you, all godfathers and godmothers, to carry out these hints of mine, and so fulfil your duty to your godchildren, sure that you will find it a blessing to yourselves as well as to them.

After all it is your duty. But do not let the slandering Devil slander to you that blessed word, Duty, and make you afraid of it, and shrink from it, as if it meant something burdensome, and troublesome, and thankless, which you suppose you must do for fear of punishment, while you have a right to see how little of it you can do, and try to be let off as cheaply as possible. Beware of that evil spirit, my friends, for he is very near you, and me, and every man, whenever we think of our duty. Very near us he is, that evil Jesuit spirit, that spirit of bondage unto fear, which is continually setting us on to find out with how little service God will be contented, how human slaves may make the cheapest bargain with some stern taskmaster above, of whom they dream. And from that temptation there is no escape, save into the blessed name of God Himself—our Father.

Our Father!—whenever you think of your duty to God or man, think but of those two words. Remember that all duty is duty to a Father; your Father; and such a Father! Who gave His only begotten Son to die for you, who showed what He was in that Son— full of goodness, perfectly loving, perfectly merciful, perfectly just; and then you will not be inclined to ask how little obedience, how little love, how little service, He will allow you to pay to Him; but how much He will help you to pay to Him. Then you will feel that His service is perfect freedom, because it is service to a Father who loves you, and will help you to do His will. Then you will feel that His commandments are not grievous, because they are a Father's commandments, because you are bound to do them, not by dread and superstition, but by gratitude, honour, affection, respect, trust. Then you will not be thinking of what punishment will come if you disobey—no, nor of what reward will come if you obey—but you will be thinking of the commandment itself, and how to carry it out most perfectly, and let the consequences take care of themselves, because you know that your Father takes care of them; that He loves you, and therefore what He commands must be good for you, utterly the best thing for you; that He only gives you a commandment because it is good for you; that you are made in God's image, and therefore God's will must be for you the path of life, the only rule by which you can prosper now and for ever.

Do try, now, all you who are godfathers and godmothers, and for once look on your duty in this light. Be sure that in trying to do your duty you will bring a blessing on yourselves, because your duty is to a Father in heaven. Be sure that, in trying to better your godchildren, you will better yourselves; in trying to teach them, you will teach yourselves; in trying to bring them to confirmation, you will indeed confirm, root, and strengthen yourselves the more deeply in all that is good; because your godchildren are indeed God's children, and whatsoever you do for them you do for His only begotten Son Jesus Christ, as He Himself says, 'Inasmuch as ye did it unto one of the least of these little ones, ye did it unto Me.' Do not be afraid of trying; you will have a hundred reasons for not trying rise in your mind, the Devil will find you a hundred lying excuses: 'It will be so difficult; and you do not like to interfere with other people's children; and you have never cared about your godchildren yet, and it will seem so odd to begin now; and the children may not listen to you; and besides, you do not know enough to teach them; you are not good scholar enough, good liver enough, you can't preach where you don't practice.' Oh, how ready the Devil is to help a man to excuses for not doing his duty; how careful he is to keep out of a man's mind the one thought which would sweep all those excuses to the wind—the thought that this same duty, which he is trying to make look so ugly, is duty to a loving Father. Do not listen to his lies; look up to your good Father in heaven; and try. It is God's will that these children should be confirmed; it is His will that you should help to bring them to confirmation; and if it is His will, He will help you to do that will of His. It may seem difficult: but try, and the difficulty will vanish, for God will make it easy for you. You may be afraid of interfering: believe that God's Spirit is working in the hearts of your godchildren, and of their parents also; and trust to God's Spirit to make them kindly and thankful to you about the matter, and glad to see that you take an interest in their children. You may seem not to know enough: O, my friends, you know enough, every one of you, if you have courage to confess how much you know. Ask God for courage to speak out, and He will give it you. And even if you are no scholar, be sure that, as the old proverb says, 'Teaching is the best way of learning.' Any parent, or godfather, or godmother, who will try to teach their children God's truth and their duty, will find that in so doing they will teach themselves even more than they teach the children. I say it because

I know it from my own experience. And for the rest, again I say, is not God your Father? Therefore, if any man be in want of wisdom, or courage, or any other heavenly gift, let him ask of God, who giveth liberally and upbraideth not, and he shall receive it. For after all, when you ask God to teach you, and strengthen you to do your duty, you do but ask Him for a part of that very inheritance which He has already given you; a part of your inheritance in that kingdom of heaven which is a kingdom of spiritual gifts and graces, into which you were baptized as well as your godchildren.

Try then, each of you, what you can do to bring your own godchildren to confirmation, and what you can do to make them fit for confirmation; for you are members one of another, and if you will act as such, you will find strength to do your duty, and a blessing in your day from that heavenly Father from whom every fatherhood in heaven and earth, and yours among the rest, is named.

SERMON VI

JUSTIFICATION BY FAITH

By grace ye are saved.

Ephesians ii. 5.

We all hold that we are justified by faith, that is, by believing; and that unless we are justified we cannot be saved. And of all men who ever believed this, perhaps those who gave us the Church Catechism believed it most strongly. Nay, some of them suffered for it; endured persecution, banishment, and a cruel death, because they would persist in holding, contrary to the Romanists, that men were justified by faith only, and not by the works of the law; and that this was one of the root-doctrines of Christianity, which if a man did not believe, he would believe nothing else rightly. Does it not seem, then, something strange that they should never in this Catechism of theirs mention one word about justifying or justification? They do not ask the child, 'How is a man justified?' that he may answer, 'By faith alone;' they do not even teach him to say, 'I am justified already. I am in a state of justification;' but not saying one word about that, they teach him to say much more—they teach him to say that he is in a state of salvation, and to thank God boldly because he is so; and then go on at once to ask him the articles of his belief. And even more strange still, they teach him to answer that question, not by repeating any doctrines, but by repeating the simple old Apostles' Creed. They do not teach him to say, as some would now-a-days, 'I believe in original sin, I believe in redemption through Christ's death, I believe in justification by faith, I believe in sanctification by the Holy Spirit,'—true as these doctrines are; still less do they bid the child say, 'I believe in predestination, and election, and effectual calling, and irresistible grace, and vicarious satisfaction, and forensic justification, and vital faith, and the three assurances.'

Whether these things be true or false, it seemed to the ancient worthies who gave us our Catechism that children had no business with them. They had their own opinions on these matters, and spoke their opinions moderately and wisely, and the sum of their opinions we have in the Thirty-nine Articles, which are not meant for children, not even for grown persons, excepting scholars and clergymen. Of course every grown person is at liberty to study them; but no one in the Church of England is required to agree to them, and to swear that they are true, except scholars at our old Universities, and clergymen, who are bound to have studied such questions. But for the rest of Englishmen all the necessary articles of belief (so the old divines considered) were contained in the simple old Apostles' Creed.

And why? Because, it seems to me, they were what Englishmen ought to be—what too many Englishmen are too apt to boast of being in these days, while they are not so, or anything like it—and that is, honest men and practical men. They had taught the children to say that they were members of Christ, children of God, and inheritors of the kingdom of heaven; and they had taught the children, when they said that, to mean what they said; for they had no notion that 'I am,' meant 'I may possibly be;' or that 'I was made,' meant 'There is a chance of my being made some time or other.' They would not have dared to teach children to say things which were most probably not true. So believing really what they taught, they believed also that the children were justified. For if a child is not justified in being a member of Christ, a child of God, and an inheritor of the kingdom of heaven, what is he justified in being? Is not that exactly the just, right, and proper state for him, and for every man?—the very state in which all men were meant originally to be, in which all men ought to have been? So they looked on these children as being in the just, right, and proper way, on which God looks with satisfaction and pleasure, and in which alone a man can do just, right, and proper things, by the Spirit of Christ, which He gives daily and hourly to those who belong to Him and trust in Him and in His Father.

But they knew that the children could only keep in this just, and right, and proper state by trusting in God, and looking up to Him daily in faith, and love, and obedience. They knew that if the children, whether for one hour or for their whole lives, lost trust in God, and began trusting in themselves, they would that very moment, then and there, become not justified at all, because they would be doing a thing which no man is justified in doing, and fall into a state into which no man is justified in remaining for one hour—that is, into an unjustifiable state of self-will, and lawlessness, and forgetfulness of who and of what they were, and of what God was to them; in one word, into a sinful state, which is not a righteous, or just, or good, or proper state for any man, but an utterly unrighteous, unjust, wrong, improper, mistaken, diseased state, which is certain to breed unrighteous, unjust, improper actions in a man, as a limb is certain to corrupt if it be cut off from the body, as a little child is certain to come to harm if it runs away from its parents, and does just what it likes, and eats whatsoever pleases its fancy. So these old divines, being practical men, said to themselves, 'These children are justified and right in being what they are, therefore our business is to keep them what they are, and we can only do that as long as they have faith in God and in His Christ.'

Now, if they had been mere men of books, they would have said to themselves, 'Then we must teach the children very exactly what faith is, that they may know how to tell true faith from false, and may be able to judge every day and hour whether they have the right sort of faith which will justify them, or some wrong sort which will not.' And many wise and good men in those times did say so, and tormented their own minds, and the minds of weak brethren, with long arguments and dry doctrines about faith, till, in their eagerness to make out what sort of thing faith ought to be, they seemed quite to forget that it must be faith in God, and so seemed to forget too who God was, and what He was like. Therefore, they ended by making people believe (as too many, I fear, do now-a-days) not that they were justified freely by the grace of God, shown forth in the life, and death, and resurrection of his Son Jesus Christ; no: but that they were justified by believing in justification by faith, and that their salvation depended not on being faithful to God and trusting in Him, but in standing up fiercely for the doctrine of justification by faith. And so they destroyed the doctrine of free grace, while they thought they were fighting for it; for they taught men not to look to God for salvation, so much as to their own faith, their own frames, and feelings, and experiences; and these, as common sense will show you, are just as much something in a man, as acts of his own, and part of him, as his good works would be; and so by making people fancy that it was having the right sort of feelings which justified them, they fell back into the very same mistake as the Papists against whom they were so bitter, namely, that it is something in a man's self which justifies him, and not simply Christ's merits and God's free grace.

But our old Reformers were of a different mind; and everlasting thanks be to Almighty God that they were so. For by being so they have made the Church of England (as I always have said, and always will say) almost the only Church in Europe, Protestant or other, which thoroughly and fully stands up for free grace, and justification by faith alone. For these old Reformers were practical men, and took the practical way. They knew, perhaps, the old proverb, 'A man need not be a builder to live in a house.' At least they acted on it, and instead of trying to make the children understand what faith was made up of, they tried to make them live in faith itself. Instead of saying, 'How shall we make the children have faith in God by telling them what faith is?' they said, 'How shall we make them have faith in God by telling them what God is?' And therefore, instead of puzzling and fretting the children's minds with any of the controversies which were then going on between Papists and Protestants, or afterwards between Calvinists and Arminians, they taught the children simply about God; who He was, and what He had done for them and all mankind; that so they might learn to love Him, and look up to Him in faith, and trust utterly to Him, and so remain justified and right, saved and safe for ever.

By doing which, my friends, they showed that they knew more about faith and about God than if they had written books on books of doctrinal arguments (though they wrote those too, and wrote them nobly and well); they showed that they had true faith in God, such trust in Him, and in the beauty and goodness, justice and love, which He had shown, that they only needed to tell the children of it, and they would trust Him too, and at once have faith in so good a God. They showed that they had such trust in the excellencies, and reasonableness, and fitness of His Gospel, that they were sure that it would come home at once to the children's hearts. They showed that they had such trust in the power of His grace, in His love for the children, in the working of His Spirit in the children, that He would bring His Gospel home to their hearts, and stir them up by the spirit of adoption to feel that they were indeed the children of God, to whom they might freely cry, 'My Father!'

And I say that they were not deceived. I say that experience has shown that they were right; that the Church Catechism, where it is really and honestly taught, gives the children an honest, frank, sober, English temper of mind which no other training which I have seen gives. I have seen, alas! Church schools fail, ere now, in training good children; but as far as I have seen, they have failed either because the Catechism was neglected for the sake of cramming the children's brains with scholarship, or because the Catechism was not honestly taught: because the words were taught by rote, but the explanations which were given of it were no explanations at all, but another doctrine, which our forefathers knew not: either Dissenting or Popish; either a religion of fancies, and feelings, and experiences, or one of superstitious notions and superstitious ceremonies which have been borrowed from the Church of Rome, and which, I trust in God, will be soon returned to their proper owner, if the free, truthful, God-trusting English spirit is to remain in our children. I know that there are good men among

Dissenters, my friends; good men among Romanists. I have met with them, and I thank God for them; and what may not be good for English children may be good for foreign ones. I judge not; to his own master each man stands or falls. But I warn you frankly, from experience (not of my own merely—Heaven forbid!—but from the experience of centuries past), that if you expect to make the average of English children good children on any other ground than the Church Catechism takes, you will fail. Of course there will be some chosen ones here and there, whose hearts God will touch; but you will find that the greater part of the children will not be made better at all; you will find that the cleverer, and more tender-hearted will be made conceited, Pharisaical, self-deceiving (for children are as ready to deceive themselves, and play the hypocrite to their own consciences, as grown people are); they will catch up cant words and phrases, or little outward forms of reverence, and make a religion for themselves out of them to drug their own consciences withal; while, when they go out into the world, and meet temptation, they will have no real safeguard against it, because whatsoever they have been taught, they have not been taught that God is really and practically their Father, and they His children.

I have seen many examples of this kind. Perhaps those who have eyes to see may have seen one or two in this very parish. Be that as it may, I tell you, my friends, that your children shall be taught the Church Catechism, with the plain, honest meaning of the words as they stand. No less: but as God shall give me grace, no more. If it be not enough for them to know that God, He who made heaven and earth, is their Father; that His Son Jesus Christ redeemed them and all mankind by being born of the Virgin Mary, suffering under Pontius Pilate, being crucified, dead, and buried, descending into hell, rising again the third day from the dead, ascending into Heaven, and sitting on the right hand of God the Father Almighty, in the intent of coming from thence to judge the living and the dead; to believe in the Holy Spirit, in the holy universal Church in which He keeps us, in the fellowship of all Saints in which He knits us together; in the forgiveness of our sins which He proclaims to us, in the resurrection of our body which He will quicken at the last day, in the life everlasting which is His life,— if, I say, this be not enough for them to believe, and on the strength thereof to trust God utterly, and so be justified and saved from this evil world, and from the doom and punishment thereof, then they must go elsewhere; for I have nothing more to offer them, and trust in God that I never shall have.

SERMON VII

DUTY AND SUPERSTITION

*Wherewith shall I come before the Lord and bow
myself before the most High God? Shall I come before
him with burnt offerings? ... Will the Lord be pleased
with thousands of rams? ... Shall I give my firstborn
for my transgression; the fruit of my body for the sin
of my soul?*

*He hath shewed thee, O man, what is good; and what
doth the Lord require of thee, but to do justly, and to
love mercy, and to walk humbly with thy God?*

Micah vi. 6-8.

There are many now-a-days who complain of that part of the Church Catechism which speaks of our duty to God and to our neighbour; and many more, I fear, who shrink from complaining of the Church Catechism, because it is part of the Prayer-book, yet wish in their secret hearts that it had said something different about Duty.

Some wonder why it does not say more about what are called 'religious duties,' and 'acts of worship,' 'mortification,' 'penitence,' and 'good works.' Others wonder no less why it says nothing about what are called 'Christian frames and feelings,' and 'inward experiences.'

For there is a notion abroad in the world, as there is in all evil times, that a man's chief duty is to save his own soul after he is dead; that his business in this world is merely to see how he can get out of it again, without suffering endless torture after his body dies. This is called superstition: anxiety about what will happen to us after we die.

Now if you look at the greater number of religious books, whether Popish or Protestant, you will find that in practice the main thing, almost the one thing, which they are meant to do, is to show the reader how he may escape Hell-torments, and reach Heaven's pleasures after he dies: not how he may do his Duty to God and his neighbour. They speak of that latter, of course: they could not be Christian books at all, thank God, without doing so; but they seem to me to tell men to do their Duty, not simply because it is right, and a blessing in itself, and worth doing for its own sake, but because a man may gain something by it after he dies. Therefore, to help their readers to gain as much as possible after they die, they are not content with the plain Duty laid down in the Bible and in the Catechism, but require of men new duties over and above; which may be all very good if they help men to do their real Duty, but are simply worth nothing if they do not.

Let me explain myself. I said just now that superstition means anxiety about what will happen to us after we die. But people commonly understand by superstition, religious ceremonies, like the Popish ones, which God has not commanded. And that is not a wrong meaning either; for people take to these ceremonies from over-anxiety about the next life. The one springs out of the other; the outward conduct out of the inward fear; and both spring alike out of a false notion of God, which the Devil (whose great aim is to hinder us from knowing our Father in Heaven) puts into men's minds. Man feels that he is sinful and unrighteous; the light of Christ in his heart shows him that, and it shows him at the same time that God is sinless and righteous. 'Then,' he says, 'God must hate sin;' and there he says true. Then steps in the slanderer, Satan, and whispers, 'But you are sinful; therefore God hates you, and wills you harm, and torture, and ruin.' And the poor man believes that lying voice, and will believe it to the end, whether he be Christian or heathen, until he believes the Bible and the Sacraments, which tell him, 'God does not hate you: He hates your sins, and loves you; He wills not your misery but your happiness; and therefore God's will, yea, God's earnest endeavour, is to raise you out of those sins of yours, which make you miserable now, and which, if you go on in them, must bring of themselves everlasting misery to you.' Of themselves; not by any arbitrary decree of God (whereof the Bible says not one single word from beginning to end), that He will inflict on you so much pain for so much sin: but by the very nature of sin; for to sin is to be parted from God, in whose presence alone is life, and therefore sin is, to be in death. Sin is, to be at war with God, who is love and peace; and therefore to be in lovelessness, hatred, war, and misery. Sin is, to act contrary to the constitution which God gave man, when He said, 'Let us make man in our image, after our likeness;' and therefore sin is a disease in human nature, and like all other diseases, must, unless it is checked, go on everlastingly and perpetually breeding weakness, pain and torment. And out of that God is so desirous to raise you, that He spared not His only begotten Son, but freely gave Him for you, if by any means He might raise you out of that death of sin to the life of righteousness—to a righteous life; to a life of Duty—to a dutiful life, like His Son Jesus Christ's life; for that must go on, if you go on in it, producing in you everlastingly and perpetually all health and strength, usefulness and happiness in this world and all worlds to come.

But men will not hear that voice. The fact is, that simply to do right is too difficult for them, and too humbling also. They are too proud to like being righteous only with Christ's righteousness, and too slothful also; and so they go about like the old Pharisees, to establish a righteousness of their own; one which will pamper their self-conceit by seeming very strange, and farfetched, and difficult, so as to enable them to thank God every day that they are not as other men are; and yet one which shall really not be as difficult as the plain homely work of being good sons, good fathers, good husbands, good masters, good servants, good subjects, good rulers. And so they go about to establish a righteousness of their own (which can be no righteousness at all, for God's righteousness is the only righteousness, and Christ's righteousness is the only pattern of it), and teach men that God does not merely require of men to do justly, and love mercy, and walk humbly with their God, but requires of them something more. But by this they deny the righteousness of God; for they make out that he has not behaved righteously and justly to men, nor showed them what is good, but has left them to find it out or invent it for themselves. For is it not establishing a righteousness of one's own, to tell people that God only requires these Ten Commandments of Christians in general, but that if any one chooses to go further, and do certain things which are not contained in the Ten Commandments, 'counsels of perfection,' as they are called, and 'good works' (as if there were no other good works in the world), and so do more than it is one's duty to do, and lead a sort of life which is called (I know not why) 'saintly' and 'angelic,' then one will obtain a 'peculiar crown,' and a higher place in Heaven than poor commonplace Christian people, who only do justly, and love mercy, and walk humbly with their God?

And is it not, on the other hand, establishing a righteousness of one's own, to say that God requires of us belief in certain doctrines about election, and 'forensic justification,' and 'sensible conversion,' and certain 'frames and feelings and experiences;' and that without all these a man has no right to expect anything but endless torture; and all the while to say little or nothing about God's requiring of men the Ten Commandments? For my part, I am equally shocked and astonished at the doctrine which I have heard round us here— openly from some few, and in practice from more than a few—that because the Ten Commandments are part of the Law, they are done away with, because we are not now under the Law but under Grace.

What do they mean? Is it not written, that not one jot or tittle of the Law shall fail; and that Christ came, not to destroy the Law, but to fulfil it? What do they mean? That it was harm to break the Ten Commandments before Christ came, but no harm to break them now? Do they mean that Jews were forbid to murder, steal, and commit adultery, but that Christians are not forbidden? One thing I am afraid they do mean, for I see them act up to it steadily enough. That Jews were forbidden to covet, but that Christians are not; that Jews might not commit fornication, but Christians may; that Jews might not lie, but Christians may; that Jews might not use false weights and measures, or adulterate goods for sale, but that Christians may. My friends, if I am asked the reason of the hypocrisy which seems the besetting sin of England, in this day;—if I am asked why rich men, even high religious professors, dare speak untruths at public meetings, bribe at elections, and go into parliament each man with a lie in his right hand, to serve neither God nor his country, but his political party and his religious sect, by conduct which he would be ashamed to employ in private life;—if I am asked why the middle classes (and the high religious professors among them, just as much as any) are given over to cheating, coveting, puffing their own goods by shameless and unmanly boasting, undermining each other by the dirtiest means, while the sons of religious professors, both among the higher and the middle classes, seem just as liable as any other young men to fall into unmanly profligacy;—if I am asked why the poor profess God's gospel and practise the Devil's works; and why, in this very parish now, there are women who, while they are drunkards, swearers, and adulteresses, will run anywhere to hear a sermon, and like nothing better, saving sin, than high-flown religious books;—if I am asked, I say, why the old English honesty which used to be our glory and our strength, has decayed so much of late years, and a hideous and shameful hypocrisy has taken the place of it, I can only answer by pointing to the good old Church Catechism, and what it says about our duty to God and to our neighbour, and declaring boldly, 'It is because you have forgotten that. Because you have despised that. Because you have fancied that it was beneath you to keep God's plain human commandments. You have been wanting to "save your souls," while you did not care whether your souls were saved alive, or whether they were dead, and rotten, and damned within you; you have dreamed that you could be what you called "spiritual," while you were the slaves of sin; you have dreamed that you could become what you call "saints," while you were not yet even decent men and women.'

And so all this superstition has had the same effect as the false preaching in Ezekiel's time had. It has strengthened the hands of the wicked, that he should not turn from his wicked way, by promising him life; and it has made the heart of the righteous sad, whom God has not made sad. Plain, respectable, God-fearing men and women, who have wished simply to do their duty where God has put them, have been told that they are still unconverted, still carnal—that they have no share in Christ—that God's Spirit is not with them—that they are in the way to endless torture: till they have been ready one minute to say, 'Let us eat and drink, for to-morrow we die'—'Surely I have cleansed my hands in vain, and washed my heart in innocency;' and the next minute to say, with Job, angrily, 'Though I die, thou shalt not take my righteousness from me! You preachers may call me what names you will; but I know that I love what is right, and wish to do my duty;' and so they have been made perplexed and unhappy, one day fancying themselves worse than they really were, and the next fancying themselves better than they really were; and by both tempers of mind tempted to disbelieve God's Gospel, and throw away the thought of vital religion in disgust.

And now people are raising the cry that Popery is about to overrun England. It may be so, my friends. If it is so, I cannot wonder at it; if it is so, Englishmen have no one to blame but themselves. And whether Popery conquers us or not, some other base superstition surely will conquer us if we go on upon our present course, and set up any new-fangled, self-invented righteousness of our own, instead of the plain Ten Commandments of God. For I tell you plainly they are God's everlasting law, the very law of liberty, wherewith Christ has made us free; and only by fulfilling them, as Christ did, can we be free—free from sin, the world, the flesh, and the Devil. For to break them is to sin: and whosoever commits sin is the slave of sin; and whosoever despises these commandments will never enjoy that freedom, but be entangled again in the yoke of bondage, and become a slave, if not to open and profligate sins, still surely to an evil and tormenting conscience, to superstitious anxieties as to whether he shall be saved or damned, which make him at last ask, 'Wherewithal shall I come before the Lord? Will the Lord be pleased with this, that and the other fantastical action, or great sacrifice of mine?' or at last, perhaps, the old question, 'Shall I give my firstborn for my transgression, the fruit of my body for the sin of my soul? Shall I cheat my own family, leave my property away from my children, desert them to shut myself up in a convent, or to attempt some great religious enterprise?'—Things which have happened a thousand times already, and worse, far worse, than them; things which will happen again, and worse, far worse than them, as soon as a hypocritical generation is seized with that dread and terror of God which is sure to arise in the hearts of men who try to invent a righteousness of their own, and who forget what God's righteousness is like, and who therefore forget what God is like, and who therefore forget what God's name is, and who therefore forget that Jesus Christ is God's likeness, and that the name of God is 'Love.'

Now, I say that the Church Catechism, from beginning to end, is the cure for this poison, and in no part more than where it tells us our duty to God and our neighbour; and that it does carry out the meaning of the text as no other writing does, which I know of, save the Bible only.

For what says the text?

'He hath showed thee, O man, what is good.'

Who has showed thee? Who but this very God, from whom thou art shrinking; to whom thou art looking up in terror, as at a hard taskmaster, reaping where He has not sown, who willeth the death of a sinner, and his endless and unspeakable torment? The very God whom thou dreadest has stooped to save and teach thee. He hath sent His only begotten Son to thee, to show thee, in the person of a man, Jesus Christ, what a perfect man is, and what He requires of thee to be. This Lord Jesus is with thee, to teach thee to live by faith in thy heavenly Father, even as He lived, and to be justified thereby, even as He was justified by being declared to be God's well-beloved Son, and by being raised from the dead. He will show thee what is good; He has shown thee what is good, when He showed thee His own blessed self, His story and character written in the four Gospels. This is thy God, and this is thy Lord and Master; not a silent God, not a careless God, but a revealer of secrets, a teacher, a guide, a 'most merciful God, who showeth to man the thing which he knew not;' that same Word of God who talked with Adam in the garden, and brought his wife to him; who called Abraham, and gave him a child; who sent Moses to make a nation of the Jews; who is the King of all the nations upon earth, and has appointed them their times and the bounds of their habitation, if haply they may feel after Him and find Him; who meanwhile is not far from any one of them, seeing that in Him they live, and move, and have their being, and are His offspring; who has not left Himself without witness, that they may know that He is one who loves, not one who hates, one who gives, not one who takes, one who has pity, not one who destroys, in that He gives them rain and fruitful seasons, filling their hearts with food and gladness. This is thy God, O man! from whose face thou desirest to flee away.

Next, 'He hath showed thee, O man.' Not merely, 'He hath showed thee, O deep philosopher, or brilliant genius;'—not merely, 'He hath showed thee, O eminent saint, or believer who hast been through many deep experiences:' but, 'He hath showed thee, O man.' Whosoever thou art, if thou be a man, subsisting like Jesus Christ the Son of Man, of a reasonable soul and human flesh; thou labourer at the plough, tradesman in thy shop, soldier in the battlefield, poor woman working in thy cottage, God hath showed thee, and thee, and thee, what is good, as surely and fully as He has shown it to scholars and divines, to kings and rulers, and the wise and prudent of the earth.

And He hath showed thee; not you. Not merely to the whole of you together; not merely to some of you so that one will have to tell the other, and the greater part know only at second-hand and by hearsay: but He hath showed to thee, to each of you; to each man, woman, and child, in this Church, alone, privately, in the depths of thy own heart, He hath showed what is good. He hath sent into thine heart a ray of The Light who lighteth every man who comes into the world. He has given to thy soul an eye by which to see that Light, a conscience which can receive what is good, and shrink from what is evil; a spiritual sense, whereby thou canst discern good and evil. That conscience, that soul's eye of thine, God has regenerated, as He declares to thee in baptism, and He will day by day make it clearer and tenderer by the quickening power of His Holy Spirit; and that Spirit will renew Himself in thee day by day, if thou askest Him, and will quicken and soften thy soul more and more to love what is good, and strengthen it more and more to hate and fly from what is evil.

Next, 'He hath showed thee, O man, what is GOOD.' Not merely what will turn away God's punishments, and buy God's rewards; not merely what will be good for thee after thou diest: but what is good, good in itself, good for thee now, and good for thee for ever; good for thee in health and sickness, joy and sorrow, life and death; good for thee through all worlds, present and to come; yea, what would be good for thee in hell, if thou couldst be in hell and yet be good. Not what is good enough for thy neighbours and not good enough for thee, good enough for sinners and not good enough for saints, good enough for stupid persons and not good enough for clever ones; but what is good in itself and of itself. The one very eternal and absolute Good which was with God, and in God, and from God, before all worlds, and will be for ever, without changing or growing less or greater, eternally The Same Good. The Good which would be just as good, and just, and right, and lovely, and glorious, if there were no world, no men, no angels, no heaven, no hell, and God were alone in his own abyss. That very good which is the exact pattern of His Son Jesus Christ, in whose likeness man was made at the beginning, God hath showed thee, O man; and hath told thee that it is neither more nor less than thy Duty, thy Duty as a man; that thy duty is thy good, the good out of which, if thou doest it, all good things such as thou canst not now conceive to thyself, must necessarily spring up for thee for ever; but which if thou neglectest, thou wilt be in danger of getting no good things whatsoever, and of having all evil things, mishap, shame, and misery such as thou canst not now conceive of, spring up for thee necessarily for ever.

This seems to me the plain meaning of the text, interpreted by the plain teaching of the rest of Scripture. Now see how the Catechism agrees with this.

It takes for granted that God has showed the child what is good: that God's Spirit is sanctifying and making good, not only all the elect people of God, but him, that one particular child; and it makes the child say so. Therefore, when it asks him, 'What is thy duty to God and to thy neighbour?' it asks him, 'My child, thou sayest that God's Spirit is with thee, sanctifying thee and showing thee what is good, tell me, therefore, what good the Holy Spirit has showed thee?—tell me what He has showed thee to be good, and therefore thy duty?'

But some may answer, 'How can you say that the Holy Spirit teaches the children their Duty, when it is their schoolmaster, or their father, who teaches them the Ten Commandments and the Catechism?'

My friends, we may teach our children the Ten Commandments, or anything else we like, but we cannot teach them that that is their duty. They must first know what Duty means at all, before they can learn that any particular things are parts of their Duty. And, believe me, neither you nor I, nor all the men in the world put together, no, nor angel, nor archangel, nor any created being, nor the whole universe, can teach one child, no, nor our own selves, the meaning of that plain word duty, nor the meaning of those two plain words, I Ought. No; that simple thought, that thought which every one of us, even the most stupid, even the most sinful has more or less, comes straight to him from God the Father of Lights, by the inspiration of the Holy Spirit of God, the Spirit of Duty, Faith, and Obedience.

For mind—when you teach a child, 'If you do this wrong thing—stealing, for instance—God will punish you: but if you are honest, God will reward you,' you are not teaching the child that it is his Duty to be honest, and his Duty not to steal. You are teaching him what is quite right and true; namely, that it is profitable for him to be honest, and hurtful to him to steal: but you are not teaching him as high a spiritual lesson as any soldier knows when he rushes upon certain death, knowing that he shall gain nothing, and may lose everything thereby, but simply because it is his Duty. You are only enticing your child to do right, and frightening him from doing wrong; quite necessary and good to be done: but if he is to be spiritually honest, honest at heart, honest from a sense of honour, and not of fear; in one word, if he is to be really honest at all, or even to try to be really honest, something must be done to that child's heart which nothing but the Spirit of God can do; he must be taught that it is his duty to be honest; that honesty is right, the perfectly right, and proper, and beautiful thing for him and for all beings, yea, for God Himself; he must be taught to love honesty, and whatsoever else is right, for its own sake, and therefore to feel it his Duty.

And I say that God does that by your children. I say that we cannot watch our children without seeing that, though there is in them, as in us, a corrupt and wilful flesh, which tempts them downward to selfish and self-willed pleasures: yet there is in them generally, more than in us their parents, a Spirit which makes them love and admire what is right, and take pleasure in it, and feel that it is good to be good, and right to do right; which makes them delight in reading and hearing of loving, and right, and noble actions; which makes them shocked, they hardly know why, at bad words, and bad conduct, and bad people. And woe to those who deaden that tenderness of conscience in their own children, by their bad examples, or by false doctrines which tell the children that they are still unregenerate, children of the Devil, not yet Christians; and who so put a stumbling-block in the way of Christ's little ones, and do despite to the Spirit of Grace by which they are sealed to the day of redemption. I see parents thinking that their children are to learn the deceitfulness of the human heart from themselves, and the working of God's Spirit from their parents; but I often think that the teachers ought to be converted indeed, that is, turned right round and become the learners instead of the teachers, and learn the workings of God's Spirit from their children, and the deceitfulness of the human heart from themselves; if at least the Lord Jesus's words have any real force or meaning at all, when He said, not, 'Except the little children be converted, and become as you,' but, 'Except ye be converted, and become as one of these little children, ye' (and not they) 'shall in no wise enter into the kingdom of heaven.'

Believe me, my friends, that your children's angels do indeed behold the face of their Father which is in heaven; that there is a direct communication between Him and them; and that the sign and proof of it is, the way in which they understand at once what you tell them of their duty, and take to it, as it were, only too readily and hopefully, and confidently, as if it were a thing natural and easy to them. Alas! it is neither natural nor easy, and they will find out that too soon by sad experience: but still, the Divine Light is there, the sense of duty is in their minds, and the law of God is written in their hearts by the Holy Spirit of God, who is sanctifying them, not merely by teaching them to hope for heaven, or to dread hell, but by showing them what is good.

And herein, I say, the simple and noble old Church Catechism, by faith in God's Spirit, does indeed perfect praise out of the mouths of babes. Without one word about rewards or punishments, heaven or hell, it begins to talk to the child, like a true English Catechism as it is, about that glorious old English key word, duty. It calls on the child to confess its own duty, and teaches it that its duty is something most human, simple, everyday, commonplace, if you will call it so. I rejoice that it is commonplace; I rejoice that in what it says about our duty to God, and to our neighbour, it says not one word about those counsels of perfection, or those frames and feelings, which depend, believe me, principally on the state of people's bodily health, on the constitution of their nerves, and the temper of their brain: but that it requires nothing except what a little child can do as well as a grown person, a labouring man as well as a divine, a plain farmer as well as the most refined, devout, imaginative lady. May God bless them all; may God help them all to do their Duty in that station of life to which it has pleased God to call them; but may God grant to them never to forget that there is but one Duty for all, and that all of them can do that Duty equally well, whatever their constitution, or scholarship, or station of life may be, provided they will but remember that God has called them to that station, and not try to invent some new and finer one for themselves; provided they remember that they are to do in that station neither more nor less than every one else is to do in theirs, namely, to do justly, to love mercy, and to walk humbly with their God.

In a word, to be perfect, even as their Father in heaven is perfect. To do justly, because God is just, faithful, and true, rewarding every man according to his works, and no partial accepter of persons; so that in every nation he that feareth God and worketh righteousness is accepted by Him.

To love mercy, because God loves mercy; to be merciful, because our Father in heaven is merciful; because He willeth not the death of a sinner, but rather that he should turn from his wickedness and live; because God came to seek and to save that which is lost, and is good to the unthankful and the evil; and because God so loved sinful man, that when man hated God, God's answer to man's hate, God's vengeance upon man's rebellion, was, to send His only-begotten Son, that whosoever believed in Him should not perish, but have everlasting life.

And to walk humbly with your God, because—and what shall I say now? Does God walk humbly? Can there be humility in God? Can God obey? And yet it must be so. If, as is most certain from Holy Scripture, man, as far as he is what man ought to be, is the image and glory of God; if man's justice ought to be a copy of God's justice, and man's mercy a copy of God's mercy, and all which is good in man a copy of something good in God: if, as is most certain, all good on earth is God's likeness, and only good because it is God's likeness, and is given by God's Spirit,—then our walking humbly with God, if it be good, must be a copy of something in God. But of what?

That, my friends, is a question which can never be answered but by those who believe in the mystery of the ever-blessed Trinity, The Father, The Son, and The Holy Ghost. It is too solemn and great a matter to be spoken of hastily at the end of a sermon. I will tell you what little I seem to see of it next Sunday, with awe and trembling, as one who enters upon holy ground. But this I will tell you, to bear in mind meanwhile, that if you wish to know or to do what is right, you must firmly believe and bear in mind this,—that God's justice is exactly like what would be just in you and me, without any difference whatsoever: that God's mercy is exactly like what would be merciful in you and me; and that, as I hope to show you next Sunday, God's humility, wonderful as it may seem, is exactly like what would be humble in you and me. For I warn you, that if you do not believe this, you will be tempted to forget God's righteousness, and to invent a righteousness of your own, which is no righteousness at all, but unrighteousness. For there can be but one righteousness—mind what I say—only one righteousness, as there can be only one truth, and only one reason. Forget that, and you will be tempted to invent for yourselves a false justice, which is dishonest and partial; a false mercy, which is cruel; a false humility, which is vain and self-conceited; and you will be tempted also, as men of all religions and denominations have been, to impute to God actions, and thoughts, and tempers, which are (as your own consciences, if you would listen to God's Word in them, would tell you) unjust, cruel, and proud; and then you will be tempted to say that things are justifiable in God, which you would not excuse in any other being, by saying: 'Of course it must be right in Him, because He is God, and can do what He will.' As if the Judge of all the earth would not do Right; as if He could be anything, or could do anything, but the Eternal Good which is His very being and essence, and which He has shown forth in His Son Jesus Christ our Lord, who went about doing good because God was with Him. We all know what the good which He did was like. Let us believe that God the Father's goodness is the same as Jesus Christ's goodness. Let us believe really what we say when we confess that Jesus was the brightness of His Father's Glory, and the express image of His Person.

SERMON VIII

SONSHIP

*Then answered Jesus, Verily, verily, I say unto you,
The Son can do nothing of Himself, but what He seeth
the Father do: for what things soever He doeth, these
also doeth the Son likewise. For the Father loveth the
Son, and sheweth Him all things that Himself doeth.
I can of mine own self do nothing: as I hear, I judge:
and my judgment is just; because I seek not mine own
will, but the will of my Father which is in Heaven.*

John v. 19, 20, 30.

This, my friends, is why man should walk humbly and obediently with his God; because humility and obedience are the likeness of the Son of God, who, though He is equal to His Father, yet to do His Father's will humbled Himself, and took on Him the form of a slave, and though He is a Son, yet learned obedience by the things which He suffered; sacrificing Himself utterly and perfectly to do the commands of His Father and our Father, of His God and our God; and sacrificing Himself to His Father not as a man merely, but as a son; not because He was in the likeness of sinful flesh, but because He was The Everlasting Son of His Father; not once only on the cross, but from all eternity to all eternity, the Lamb slain before the foundation of the world. This is a great mystery; we may understand somewhat more of it by thinking over the meaning of those great words, Father and Son.

Now, first, a son must be of the same nature as his father,—that is certain. Each kind of animal brings forth after its kind: the lion begets lions, the sheep, sheep; the son of a man must be a man, of one substance with his earthly father; and by the same law, the Son of God must be God. Take away that notion: say that the only-begotten Son of God is not very God of very God, of one substance with His Father, and the word son means nothing. If a son be not of the same substance as his father, he is not a son at all. And more, a perfect son must be as great and as good as his father, exactly like his father in everything. That is the very meaning of father and son; that like should beget like. Among fallen and imperfect men, some sons are worse and weaker than their fathers: but we all feel that that is an evil, a thing to be sorry for, a sad consequence of our fallen state. Our reasons and hearts tell us that a son ought to be equal to his father, and that it is in some way an affliction, almost a shame, to a father, if his children are weaker or worse than he is. But we cannot fancy such a thing in God; the only-begotten perfect Son of the Almighty and perfect Father must be at least equal to His Father, as great as His Father, as good as His Father; the brightness of His Father's glory, and the express image of His Father's person.

But there is another thing about father and son which we must look at, and that is this: a good son loves and obeys his father, and the better son he is, the more he loves and obeys his father; and therefore a perfect son will perfectly love and perfectly obey his father.

Now, here is the great difference between animals and men. Among the higher animals, the mothers always, and the fathers sometimes, feed, and help, and protect their young: but we seldom or never find that young animals help and protect their parents; certainly, they never obey their fathers when they are full grown, but are as ready to tear their fathers in pieces as their fathers are to tear them: so that the love and obedience of full-grown sons to their fathers is so utterly human a thing, so utterly different from anything we find in the brutes, that we must believe it to be part of man's immortal soul, part of God's likeness in man.

And in the text our Lord declares that it is so; He declares that His obedience to His Father, and His Father's love to Him, is the perfect likeness of what goes on between a good son and a good father among men; only that it is perfect, because it is between a perfect Father and a perfect Son.

Father and Son! Let philosophers and divines discover what they may about God, they will never discover anything so deep as the wonder which lies in those two words, Father and Son. So deep, and yet so simple! So simple, that the wayfaring man, though poor, shall not err therein. 'Who is God? What is God like? Where shall we find Him, or His likeness?'—so has mankind been crying in all ages, and getting no answer, or making answers for themselves in all sorts of superstitions, idolatries, false philosophies. And then the Gospel comes, and answers to every man, to every poor and unlearned labourer: Will you know the name of God? It is a Father, a Son, and a Holy Spirit of love, joy, peace; a Spirit of perfect satisfaction of the Father in the Son, and perfect satisfaction of the Son with the Father, which proceeds from both the Father and the Son. It needs no scholarship to understand that Name; every one may understand it who is a good father; every one may understand it who is a good son, who looks up to and obeys his father with that filial spirit of love, and obedience, and satisfaction with his father's will, which is the likeness of the Holy Spirit of God, and can only flourish in any man by the help of the Holy Spirit which proceeds from the Father and the Son.

Father and Son! what more beautiful words are there in the world? What more beautiful sight is there in the world than a son who really loves his father, really trusts his father, really does his duty to his father, really looks up to and obeys his father's will in all things? who is ready to sacrifice his own credit, his own pleasure, his own success in life, for the sake of his father's comfort and honour? How much more fair and noble must be the love and trust which is between God the Father and God the Son!

I wish that some of those who now write so many excellent books for young people, would write one made up entirely of stories of good sons who have obeyed, and worked for, and suffered for their parents. Sure I am that such a book, wisely and well written, would teach young people much of the meaning of the blessed name of God, much of their duty to God. And yet, after all, my friends, is not such a book written already? Have we not the four Gospels, which tell us of Jesus Christ, the perfect Son, who came to do the will of a perfect Father? Read that; read your Bibles. Read the history of the Lord Jesus Christ, keeping in mind always that it is the history of the Son of God, and of His obedience to His Father. And when in St. John's most wonderful Gospel you meet with deep texts, like the one which I have chosen, read them too as carefully, if possible more carefully, than the rest; for they are meant for all parents and for all children upon earth. Read how The Father loves The Son, and gives all things into His hand, and commits all judgment to The Son, and gives Him power to have life in Himself, even as The Father has life in Himself, and shows Him all things that Himself doeth, that all men may honour The Son even as they honour The Father. Read how The Son came only to show forth His Father's glory; to be the brightness of His glory and the express image of His person: to establish His Father's kingdom; to declare the goodness of His Father's Name, which is The Father. How He does nothing of Himself, but only what He sees His Father do; how He seeks not His own will, but the will of the Father who sent Him; how He sacrificed all, yea even His most precious body and soul upon the cross, to finish the work which His Father gave Him to do. How, being in the form of God, and thinking it no robbery to be equal with God, He could boldly say, 'As the Father knoweth me, even so know I the Father. I and my Father are one:' and still, in the fulness of His filial love and obedience, declared that He had no will, no wish, no work, no glory, but His Father's; and in the hour of His agony cried out, 'Father, if it be possible, let this cup pass from me: nevertheless, not my will but thine be done.'

My friends, you will be able to understand more and more of the meaning of these words just in proportion as you are good sons and good fathers; and therefore, just in proportion as you are led and taught by the Holy Spirit of God, without whose help no man can be either a good father or a good son. A bad son; a disobedient, self-willed, self-conceited son, who is seeking his own credit and not his father's, his own pleasure and not his parent's comfort; a son who is impatient of being kept in order and advised, who despises his parent's counsel, and will have none of his reproof,—to him these words of our Lord, the deepest, noblest words which were ever spoken on earth, will have no more meaning than if they were written in a foreign language; he will not know what our Lord means; he will not be able to see why our Lord came and suffered; he will not see any beauty in our Lord's character, any righteousness in His sacrificing Himself for His Father; and because he has forgotten his duty to his earthly father, he will never learn his duty to God.

For what is the duty of the Lord Jesus Christ is our duty, if we are the sons of God in Him. He is The Son of God by an eternal never-ceasing generation; we are the sons of God by adoption. The way in which we are to look up to God, The Holy Spirit must teach us; what is our duty to God The Holy Spirit must teach us. And who is The Holy Spirit? He is The Spirit who proceeds from The Son as well as from The Father. He is The Spirit of Jesus Christ, The Spirit of the Son of God, the Spirit who descended on the Lord Jesus when He was baptized, the Spirit which God gave to Him without measure. He is the Spirit of The Son of God; and we are sons of God by adoption, says Saint Paul; and because we are sons, he says, God has sent forth into our hearts the Spirit of His Son, by whom we look up to God as our Father; and this Spirit of God's Son, by whom we cry to God, Abba, Father, St. Paul calls, in another place, the Spirit of adoption; and declares openly that He is the very Spirit of God.

Therefore, in whatsoever way the Spirit of God is to teach you to look up to God, He will teach you to look up to Him as a Father; the Father of Spirits, and therefore your Father; for you are a spirit. Whatsoever duty to God the Holy Spirit teaches you, He teaches you first, and before all things, that it is filial duty, the duty of a son to a father, because you are the son of God, and God is your Father.

Therefore, whatsoever man or book tells you that your duty to God is anything but the duty of a son to his father does not speak by the Spirit of God. Whatsoever thoughts or feelings in your own hearts tell you that your duty to God is anything but the duty of a son to his father, and tempt you to distrust God's forgiveness, and shrink from Him, and look up to Him as a taskmaster, and an austere and revengeful Lord, are not the Spirit of God; no, nor your own spirit, 'the spirit of a man,' which is in you; for that was originally made in the likeness of God's Spirit, and by it rebellious sons arise and go back to their earthly fathers, and trust in them when they have nothing else left to trust, and say to themselves, 'Though all the world has cast me off, my parents will not. Though all the world despise and hate me, my parents love me still; though I have rebelled against them, deserted them, insulted them, I am still my father's child. I will go home to my own people, to the house where I was born, to the parents who nursed me on their knee, I will go to my father.'

Fathers and mothers! if your son or daughter came home to you thus, though they had insulted you, disgraced you, and spent their substance in riotous living, would you shut your doors upon them? Would not all be forgiven and forgotten at once? Would not you call your neighbours to rejoice with you, and say, 'It is good to be merry and glad, for this our son was dead and is alive again, he was lost and is found?' And would not that penitent child be more precious to you, though you cannot tell why, than any other of your children? Would you not feel a peculiar interest in him henceforth? And do you not know that so to forgive would be no weak indulgence, but the part of a good father; a good, and noble, and human thing to do? Ay, a human thing, and therefore a divine thing, part of God's likeness in man. For is it not the likeness of God Himself? Has not God Himself, in the Parable of the Prodigal Son, declared that He does so forgive His penitent children, at once and utterly, and that 'There is more joy among the angels of God over one sinner that repenteth, than over ninety and nine just persons who need no repentance?' So says the Lord Jesus Christ, the only begotten Son of God. Let who dare dispute His words, or try to water them down, and explain them away.

And why should it not be so? Do you fancy God less of a father than you are? Is He not The Father, the perfect Father, 'from whom every fatherhood in heaven and earth is named?' Oh, believe that He is indeed a Father; believe that all the love and care which you can show to your children is as much poorer than the love and care God shows to you, as your obedience to your earthly parents is poorer and weaker than the love and obedience of Jesus Christ to His Father. God is as much better a Father than you are, as Jesus

Christ is a better Son than you are. There is a sum of proportions; a rule-of-three sum; work it out for yourselves, and then distrust God's love if you dare.

And believe, that whatsoever makes you distrust God's love is neither the Spirit of God who is the spirit of sonship, nor the spirit of man: but the spirit of the Devil, who loves to slander God to men, that they may shrink from Him, and be afraid to arise and go to their Father, to be received again as sons of God; that so, being kept from true penitence, they may be kept from true holiness, and from their duty to God, which is the duty of sons of God to their Father in heaven.

Believe no such notions, my friends; howsoever humble and reverent they may seem, they are but insults to God; for under pretence of honouring Him, they dishonour Him; for He is love, and he who feareth, that is, who looks up to God with terror and distrust, is not made perfect in love. So says St. John, in the very chapter wherein he tells us that God is love, and has manifested His love to us by sending His Son to be the Saviour of the world; and that the very reason for our loving God is, that He loves us already; and that therefore He who loveth not knoweth not God, for God is love.

Yes, my friends, God is your Father; and God is love; and your duty to God is a duty of love and obedience to a Father who so loved you and all mankind that He spared not His only begotten Son, but freely gave Him for you. 'Our Father which art in heaven,' is to be the key-note of all your duty, as it is to be the key-note of all your prayers: and therefore the Catechism is right in teaching the child that God is his Father, and Jesus Christ the perfect Son of God his pattern, and the Holy Spirit of the Father and of the Son his teacher and inspirer, before it says one word to the child about duty to God, or sin against God. How indeed can it tell him what sin is, until it has told him against whom sin is committed, and that if he sins against God he sins against a Father, and breaks his duty to his Father? And how can it tell him that till it has told him that God is his Father? How can it tell him what sin is till it has told him what righteousness is? How can it tell him what breaking his duty is till it has told him what the duty itself is? But the child knows already that God is his Father; and therefore, when the Catechism asks him, 'What is his duty to God?' it is as much as to say, 'My child, thou hast confessed already that thou hast a good Father in heaven, and thou knowest as well as I (perhaps better) what a father means. Tell me, then, how dost thou think thou oughtest to behave to such a Father?' And the whole answer which is put into the child's mouth, is the description of duty to a father; of things which there would be no reason for his doing to anyone who was not his father; nay, which he could not do honestly to anyone else, but only hypocritically, for the sake of flattering, and which differs utterly from any notion of duty to God which the heathen have ever had just in this, that it is a description of how a son should behave to a father. Read it for yourselves, my friends, and judge for yourselves; and may God give you all grace to act up to it—not in order that you, by 'acts of faith,' or 'acts of love,' or 'acts of devotion,' may persuade God to love you; but because He loves you already, with a love boundless as Himself; because in Him you live, and move, and have your being, and are the offspring of God; because His mercy is over all His works, and because He loved the world, and sent His Son, not to condemn the world, but that the world through Him might be saved; because He is The Giver, The Father of lights, from whom comes every good and perfect gift; because all which makes this earth habitable—all justice, order, wisdom, goodness, mercy, humbleness, self-sacrifice—all which is fair, or honourable, or useful, in men or angels, in kings on their thrones or in labourers at the plough, in divines in their studies or soldiers in the field of battle—all in the whole universe, which is not useless, and hurtful, and base, and damnable, and doomed (blessed thought that it is so!) to be burned up in unquenchable fire—all, I say, comes forth from the Father of the spirits of all flesh, the Lord of Hosts, who is wonderful in counsel and excellent in working; who spared not His only begotten Son, but freely gave Him for us, and will with Him freely give us all things.

SERMON IX

THE LORD'S PRAYER

*After this manner pray ye: Our Father which art in
heaven.*

Matt. vi. 9, 10.

I have shown you what a simple account of our duty to God and
to our neighbour the Catechism gives us. I now beg you to remark,
that simple and everyday as this same duty is, the Catechism warns
us that we cannot do it without God's special grace, and I beg you to
remark further, that the Catechism does not say that we cannot do
these things well without God's special grace, but that we cannot do
them at all. It does not say that we cannot do all these things of
ourselves, but that we can do none of them. But I want you to
remark one thing more, which is very noteworthy: that in this case,
for the first time throughout the Catechism, the teacher tells the
child something. All along the teacher has, as I have often shown
you, been making the child tell him what is right, calling out in the
child's heart thoughts and knowledge which were there already.
Now he in his turn tells the child something which he takes for
granted is not in the child's heart, of which, if it is, has been put into
it by his teachers, and of which he must be continually reminded,
lest he should forget it; namely, that he cannot do these of himself;
that, as St. Paul says, 'in him,' that is, in his flesh, 'dwells no good
thing;' that he is not able to think or to do anything as of himself,
but his sufficiency is of God, who works in him to will and to do of
His good pleasure, who has also given him His Holy Spirit.

The Catechism, in short, takes for granted that the child knows
his duty; but it takes for granted also that he does not know how to
do that duty. It takes for granted, that in every child there is as St.
Paul says, 'a law in his members warring against the law of his
mind, and bringing him into captivity to the law of sin' (literally, of
short coming, or missing the mark) 'which is in his members.' Now
man's natural inclination is to suppose that good thoughts are part
of himself, and therefore that a good will to put them in practice is
in his own power. I blame no one for making that mistake: but I
warn them, in the name of the Bible and of the Catechism, that it is
a mistake, and one which every man, woman, and child will surely

discover to be a mistake, if they try to act on it. Good thoughts are not our own; they are Jesus Christ's; they come from Him, The Life and The Light of men; they are His voice speaking to our hearts, informing us of His laws, showing us what is good. And good desires are not our own: they come from the Holy Spirit of God, who strives with men, and labours to lift their hearts up from selfishness to love; from what is low and foul, to what is noble and pure; from what is sinful and contrary to God's will, to what is right and according to God's will.

This is the lesson which you and I and every man have to learn: that in ourselves dwells no good thing; but that there is One near us mightier than we, from whom all good things do come; and that He loves us, and will not only teach us what is good, but give us the power to do the good we know. But if we forget that, if we take any credit whatsoever to ourselves for the good which comes into our minds, then we shall be surely taught our mistake by sore afflictions and by shameful falls; by God's leaving us to ourselves, to try our own strength, and to find it weakness; to try our own wisdom, and find it folly; to try our own fancied love of God, and find that after all our conceit of ourselves, we love ourselves better, when it comes to a trial, than we love what is right; until, in short, we are driven with St. Paul to feel that, howsoever much our hearts may delight in the Law of God, there is a corrupt nature in us which fights against our delight in God's law, and will surely conquer it, and make us slaves to our own fancies, slaves to our passions, slaves to ourselves, ay, slaves to the very lowest and meanest part of ourselves: unless we can find a deliverer; unless we can find some one stronger than us, who can put an end to this hateful, shameful war within us between good wishes and bad deeds.

And then, if we will but cry with St. Paul, 'Oh, wretched man that I am, who shall deliver me from the body of this death?' we shall surely, sooner or later, hear a voice within our hearts, a voice full of love, of comfort, of fellow-feeling for us,—'I will deliver thee, my child; I, even I thy Father in heaven; I will teach thee, and inform thee in the way wherein thou shouldest go; and I will guide thee with mine eye.' And then with St. Paul we shall be able to answer our own question, and say, 'Who will deliver me? I thank God, that God Himself will deliver me, through Jesus Christ our Lord.'

This, then, is the reason why we need to pray: because we need to be delivered from ourselves. This is the reason why we may pray, because God is willing to deliver us from ourselves, if we be willing.

But every human being round us needs to be delivered from themselves, just as much as we do. Without that deliverance we cannot do our duty, neither can they. And just in proportion as men are delivered from themselves, will mankind do its duty, and the world go right.

Now their duty is the same as ours; and therefore the prayer which is right and good for us is equally right and good for them. And what is more, we cannot pray rightly for ourselves unless we pray for them in the very same breath; for the Catechism tells us that there is one duty for all of us, to love and obey and serve our heavenly Father, and to love our neighbour as ourselves, because they are our brothers, children of one common Father, members of the same God's family as we are, and their interest and ours are bound up together. Yes, to love all mankind as ourselves; for though too many of them, alas! are not yet in God's family, and strangers to His covenant, yet God's will is that they too should come to the knowledge of the truth; and therefore for them we can pray hopefully and trustfully, 'Lord have mercy on all men, on Jews, Turks, Infidels, and heretics; and bring them home, blessed Lord, to Thy flock, that they may be saved and made one fold under one Shepherd, through Jesus Christ our Lord, in whom Thou hast declared Thy good will to all the children of men.'

This is the right prayer. That all men may do their duty where God has put them. That those who, like the heathen, do not know their duty, may be taught it; that we who do know it, may have strength to do it.

And therefore it is that the Catechism teaches us the need of prayer, immediately after making us confess our duty; and therefore it is that it begins by teaching the Lord's Prayer, because that prayer is the one, of all prayers which ever have been offered upon earth, which perfectly expresses the duty of man, and man's relation to Almighty God.

It is throughout a prayer for strength. It confesses throughout what we want strength for, to what use we are to put God's grace if He bestows it on us. Our delight in the Lord's Prayer will depend on what we consider our duty here on earth to be.

If we look upon this earth principally as a place where we are to pray for all the good things which we can get, our first prayer will be, of course, 'Give us this day our daily bread.'

If we look at this earth principally as a place where we have a chance of being saved from punishment and torment after we die, then our first prayer will be, 'Forgive us our sins.' And, in fact, that is all that too many of our prayers now-a-days seem to consist of,— 'Oh, my Maker, give me. my daily bread. Oh, my Judge, forgive me my sins.' Right prayers enough, but spoilt by being taken out of their place; spoilt by being prayed before all other prayers; spoilt, too, by being prayed for ourselves alone, and not for other people also.

But if we believe, as the Bible and the Catechism tell us, that we and all Christian people are God's children, members of God's family, set on earth in God's kingdom to do His work by doing our duty, each in that station of life to which God has called us, in the hope of a just reward hereafter according to our works, then our great desire will be for strength to do our duty, and the Lord's Prayer will seem to us the most perfect way of asking for that strength; and if we believe that we are God's children and He our Father, we shall feel sure that we must get strength from Him, and sure that we must ask for that strength; and sure that He will give it us if we do ask.

But if His will is to give it us, why ask Him at all? Why pray at all, if God already knows our necessities, and is able and willing to supply them?

My friends, the longer I live, the more certain I am that the only reason for praying at all is because God is our Father; the more certain I am that we shall never have any heart to pray unless we believe that God is our Father. If we forget that, we may utter to Him selfish cries for bread; or when we look at His great power, we may become terrified, and utter selfish cries to Him not to harm us, without any real shame or sorrow for sin: but few of us will have any heart to persevere in those cries. People will say to themselves, 'If God is evil, He will not care to have mercy on me: and if He is good, there is no use wearying Him by asking Him what He has already intended to give me: why should I pray at all?'

The only answer is, 'Pray, because God is your Father, and you His child.' The only answer; but the most complete answer. I will engage to say, that if anyone here is ever troubled with doubts about prayer, those two simple words, 'Our Father,' if he can once really believe them in their full richness and depth, will make the doubts vanish in a moment, and prayer seem the most natural and reasonable of all acts. It is because we are God's children, not merely His creatures, that He will have us pray. Because He is educating us to know Him; to know Him not merely to be an Almighty Power, but a living, loving Person; not merely an irresistible Fate, but a Father who delights in the love of His children, who wishes to shape them into His own likeness, and make them fellow-workers with Him; therefore it is that He will have us pray. Doubtless he could have given us everything without our asking; for He does already give us almost everything without our asking. But He wishes to educate us as His children; to make us trust in Him; to make us love Him; to make us work for Him of our own free wills, in the great battle which He is carrying on against evil; and that He can only do by teaching us to pray to Him. I say it reverently, but firmly. As far as we can see, God cannot educate us to know Him, The living, willing, loving Father, unless He teaches us to open our hearts to Him, and to ask Him freely for what we want, just because He knows what we want already.

If I have not made this plain enough to any of you, my friends, let me go back to the simple, practical explanation of it which God Himself has given us in those two words—father and child.

Should you like to have a child who never spoke to you, never asked you for anything? Of course not. And why? 'Because,' you would say, 'one might as well have a dumb animal in one's family instead of a child, if it is never to talk and ask questions and advice.' Most true and reasonable, my friends. And as you would say concerning your children, so says God of His. You feel that unless you teach your children to ask you for all they want, even though you know their necessities before they ask, and their ignorance in asking, you will never call out their love and trust towards you. You know that if you want really to have your child to please and obey you, not as a mere tame animal, but as a willing, reasonable, loving child, you must make him know that you are training him; and you must teach him to come to you of his own accord to be trained, to be taught his duty, and set right where he is wrong: and even so does God with you. If you will only consider the way in which any child must be educated by its human parents, then you will at once see why prayer to our Heavenly Father is a necessary part of our education in the kingdom of heaven.

Now the Lord's Prayer, just this sort of prayer, is man's cry to his Heavenly Father to train him, to educate him, to take charge of him, daily and hourly, body and soul and spirit. It is a prayer for grace, for special grace; that is, for help, daily and hourly, in each particular duty and circumstance; for help from God specially suited to enable us to do our duty. And the whole of the prayer is of this kind, and not, as some think, the latter part only.

It is too often said that the three first sentences are not prayers for man, but rather praises to God. My friends, they cannot be one without being the other. You cannot, I believe, praise God aright without praying for men; you cannot pray for men aright without praising God; at least, you cannot use the Lord's Prayer without doing both at once, without at once declaring the glory of God and praying for the welfare of all mankind.

'Hallowed be Thy name.' Is not that a prayer for men as well as praise to God? Yes, my friends, when you say, 'Our Father, hallowed be Thy name,' you pray that all men may come at last to look up to God as their Father, to love, serve, and obey God as His children; and for what higher blessing can you pray? Ay, and you pray, too, that men may learn at last the deep meaning of that word—father; that they may see how Godlike and noble a trust God lays on them when He gives them children to educate and make Christian men; you pray that the hearts of all fathers may be turned to the children, and the hearts of all children to the fathers; you pray for the welfare, and the holiness, and the peace of every home on earth; you pray for the welfare of generations yet unborn, when you pray, 'Our Father, hallowed be Thy name.'

'Thy kingdom come.' Is not that too, if we will look at it steadfastly, prayer for our neighbours, prayer for all mankind, and still prayer for ourselves; prayer for grace, prayer for the life and health of our own souls?

'Thy kingdom come.'—That kingdom of the Father which Jesus Christ proved by His works on earth to be a kingdom of justice and righteousness, of love and fellow-feeling. When we pray, 'Thy kingdom come,' it is as if we said, 'Son of God, root out of this sinful earth all self-will and lawlessness, all injustice and cruelty; root out all carelessness, ignorance, and hardness of heart; root out all hatred, envy, slander; root them out of all men's hearts; out of my heart, for I have the seeds of them in me. Make me, and all men round me, day by day, more sure that Thou art indeed our King; that Thou hast indeed taught us the laws of Thy Father's kingdom; and that, only in keeping them and loving them is there health, and righteousness, and safety for any soul of man, for any nation under the sun.' 'Thy will be done;'—no, not merely 'Thy will be done;' but done 'on earth as it is in heaven;' done, not merely as the trees and the animals, the wind and clouds, do Thy will, by blindly following their natures, but done as angels and blessed spirits do it, of their own will. They obey Thee as living, willing, loving persons; as Thy sons: teach us to obey Thee in like manner; lovingly, because we love Thy will; willingly, because our wills are turned to Thy will; and therefore, oh Heavenly Father, take charge of these wayward wills and minds of ours, of these selfish, self-willed, ignorant, hasty hearts of ours, and cleanse them and renew them by Thy Spirit, and change them into Thy likeness day by day. Make us all clean hearts, oh God, and renew within us a right spirit, the copy of Thine own Holy Spirit. Cast us not away from Thy presence, for from Thee alone comes our soul's life; take not from us Thy Holy Spirit, who is The Lord and Giver of Life; whose will is Thy will; who alone can strengthen and change us to do Thy will on earth, as saints and angels do in heaven, and to be fellow-workers with each other, fellow-workers with Thee, O God, even as those blessed spirits are who minister day and night to all Thy creatures.

'Give us this day our daily bread.' People sometimes divide the Lord's Prayer into two parts—the ascriptions and the petitions—and consider that after we have sufficiently glorified and praised God in the first three sentences of the prayer, then we are at liberty to begin asking something for ourselves, and to say 'Give us day by day our daily bread.' I cannot think so, my friends. I have been showing you that 'Hallowed be Thy name, Thy kingdom come, Thy will be done,' if we do but recollect that they are spoken to our Father, are just as much prayers for all mankind, as they are hymns of honour to God; and so I say of these latter: 'Give us—Forgive us—Lead us not—Deliver us'—that if we will but remember that they, too, are spoken to our Father, we shall find that they are just as much hymns of honour to God as prayers for mankind.

Yes, my friends, when we say, 'Give us this day our daily bread,' we do indeed honour God and the name of God. We declare that He is Love, that He is The Giver, The absolutely and boundlessly generous and magnanimous Being. And what higher glory and honour or praise can we ascribe, even to God Himself, than to say that of Him? Next, we pray not for ourselves only, but for our neighbours; for England, for Christendom, for the heathen who know not God, and for generations yet unborn. We pray that God would so guide, and teach, and preserve the children of men, as to enable them to fulfil in every country and every age the work which He gave them to do, when He said, 'Be fruitful, and multiply, and fill the earth, and subdue it.' We know that our Father has commanded us to labour. We know that our Father has so well ordered this glorious earth, that whosoever labours may reap the just fruit of his labour; therefore we pray that God would prosper our righteous plans for earning our own living. We pray to Him not only so to order the earth that it may bring forth its fruits in due season, but that men may be in a fit state to enjoy those fruits, that God may not be forced for their good to withhold from them blessings which they might abuse to their ruin. But we pray, also, 'Give us:' not me only, but us; and therefore we pray that He would prosper our neighbour's plans as well as ours. So we confess that we believe God to be no respecter of persons; we confess that we believe He will not take bread out of others' mouths to give it to us; we declare that God's curse is on all selfishness and oppression of man by man; we renounce our own selfishness, the lust which our fallen nature has to rise upon others' fall, and say, 'Father, we are all children at Thy common table. Thou alone canst prosper the richest and the wisest; Thou alone canst prosper the poorest and the weakest; Thou wilt do equal justice to all some day, and we confess that Thou art just in so doing; we only ask Thee to do it now, and to give us and all mankind that which is good for them.'

Thus we pray not for this generation only, but for generations yet unborn; not for this nation of England only, but for heathens and savages beyond the seas. When we say, 'Give us our daily bread,' we pray for every child here and on earth, that he may receive such an education as may enable him to get his daily bread. We pray for learned men in their studies, that they may discover arts and sciences which shall enrich and comfort nations yet unborn. We pray for merchants on the seas, that they may discover new markets for trade, new lands to colonize and fill with Christian men, and extend the blessings of industry and civilization to the savage who lives as the beasts which perish and dwindles down off the face of the earth by famine, disease, and war, the victim of his own idleness, ignorance, and improvidence.

And all the while we are praying for the widow and the orphan, that God would send them friends in time of need; for the houseless wanderer, for the shipwrecked sailor, for sick persons, for feeble infants, that God would send help to them who cannot help themselves, and soften our hearts and the hearts of all around us, that we may never turn our faces away from any poor man, lest the face of the Lord be turned away from us.

So far we have been praying to our Heavenly Father, first as a Father, then as a King, then as an Inspirer, then as a Giver; and next we pray to Him as a Forgiver—'Forgive us our trespasses.' We have been confessing in these four petitions what God's goodwill to man is; what God wishes man to be, how man ought to live and believe. And then comes the recollection of sin. We must confess what God's law is before we can confess that we have broken it; and now we do confess that we have broken it. We know that God is our Father. How often have we forgotten that He is a father; how often have we forgotten to be good fathers ourselves.

We are in God's kingdom. How often have we behaved as if we were our own kings, and had no masters over us but our own fancies, tempers, appetites! We are to do His will on earth as it is done in heaven. How have we been doing our own will!—pleasing ourselves, breaking loose from His laws, trying to do right of our own wills and in our own strength, instead of asking His Spirit to strengthen, and cleanse, and renew our wills, and so have ended by doing not the right which we knew to be right, but the wrong which we knew to be wrong. God is a giver. How often have we looked on ourselves as takers, and fancied that we must as it were steal the good things of this world from God, lest He should forget to give us what was fitting! How often have we forgotten that God gives to all men, as well as to us; and while we were praying, give me my daily bread, kept others out of their daily bread!

Oh, my friends, we cannot blame ourselves too much for all these sins; we cannot think them too heinous. We cannot confess them too openly; we cannot cry too humbly and earnestly for forgiveness. But we never shall feel the full sinfulness of sin; we never shall thoroughly humble ourselves in confession and repentance, unless we remember that all our sins have been sins against a Father, and a forgiving Father, and that it is His especial glory, the very beauty and excellence in Him, which ought to have kept us from disobeying Him, that He does forgive those who disobey Him.

And, lastly, in like manner, when you say, 'Lead us not into temptation, but deliver,' &c., you are not only entreating God to lead you, but you are honouring and praising Him, you are setting forth His glory, and declaring that He is a God who does lead, and a God who does not leave His poor creatures to wander their own foolish way, but guides men, in spite of all their sins, full of condescension and pity, care and tender love. You do not only ask God to deliver you from evil, but you declare that He is righteous, and hates evil; that He is love, and desires to deliver you from evil; One who spared not His only-begotten Son, but gave Him freely for us, to deliver us from evil; and raised Him up, and delivered all power into His hand, that He might fight His Father's battle against all which is hurtful to man and hateful to God, till death itself shall be destroyed, and all enemies put under the feet of the Saviour God.

SERMON X

THE DOXOLOGY

*O Lord our Governor, how excellent is Thy name in
all the earth, Thou that hast set Thy glory above the
heavens!*
*Out of the mouth of babes and sucklings hast Thou
ordained strength, because of Thine enemies, that
Thou mightest still the enemy and the avenger.*

Psalm viii. 1 and sqq.

This is the text which I have chosen to-day, because I think it
will help us to understand the end of the Lord's Prayer, which tells
us to say to our Father in Heaven, 'Father, Thine is the kingdom;
Father, Thine is the power; Father, Thine is the glory.'

The man who wrote this psalm had been looking up at the sky,
spangled with countless stars, with the moon, as if she were the
queen of them all, walking in her brightness. He had been looking
round, too, on this wonderful earth, with its countless beasts, and
birds, and insects, trees, herbs, and flowers, each growing, and
thriving, and breeding after their kind, according to the law which
God had given to each of them, without any help of man. And then
he had thought of men, how small, weak, ignorant, foolish, sinful
they were, and said to himself, 'Why should God care for men more
than for these beasts, and birds, and insects round? Not because he
is the largest and strongest thing in the world; for I will consider
Thy heavens, even the work of Thy hands, the moon and the stars,
which Thou hast ordained, how much greater, more beautiful they
are than poor human beings. May not glorious beings, angels, be
dwelling in them, compared to whom man is no better than a
beast?'

And yet he says to himself, 'I know that God, though He has put
man lower than the angels, has crowned him with glory and honour.
I know that, whatever glorious creatures may live in the sun, and
moon, and stars, God has given man the dominion and power here,
on this world. I know that even to babes and sucklings God has
given a strength, because of His enemies—that He may silence the
enemy and the avenger; and I know that by so doing, God has set

His glory above the heavens, and has shown forth His glory more in these little children, to whom He gives strength and wisdom, than He has in sun, and moon, and stars.'

Now how is that? The Catechism, I think, will tell us. The Doxology, at the end of the Lord's Prayer, will tell us, if we consider it.

If you will listen to me, I will try and show you what I mean.

Suppose I took one of your children, and showed him that large bright star, which you may see now every evening, shining in the south-west, and said to him, 'My child, that star, which looks to you only a bright speck, is in reality a world—a world fourteen hundred times as big as our world. We have but one moon to light our earth; that little speck has four moons, each of them larger than ours, which light it by night. That little speck of a star seems to you to be standing still; in reality, it is travelling through the sky at the rate of 25,000 miles an hour.' What do you think the child's feeling would be? If he were a dull child, he might only be astonished; but if he were a sensible and thoughtful child, do you not think that a feeling of awe, almost of fear, would come over him, when he thought how small and weak and helpless he was, in comparison of those mighty and glorious stars above his head?

And next, if I turned the child round, and bade him look at that comet or fiery star, which has appeared lately low down in the north-west, and said, 'My child, that comet, which seems to you to hang just above the next parish, is really eighty millions of miles off from us. That bright spot at the lower part of it is a fiery world as large as the moon,—that tail of fiery light which you see streaming up from it, and which looks a few feet long, is a stream of fiery vapour, stretching, most likely, hundreds of thousands of miles through the boundless space. It seems to you to be sinking behind the trees, so slowly that you cannot see it move. It is really rushing towards us now, with its vast train of light, at the rate of some eighty thousand miles an hour.' And suppose then, if, to make the child more astonished than ever, I went on—'Yes, my child, every single tiny star which is twinkling over your head is a sun, a sun as large, or larger than our own sun, perhaps with worlds moving round it, as our world moves round our sun, but so many millions of miles far off, that the strongest spy-glass cannot make these stars look any larger, or show us the worlds which we believe are moving round them.'

Do you not think that just in proportion to the child's quickness and understanding, he would be awed, almost terrified?

And lastly, suppose that to puzzle and astonish him still more, I took a chance drop of water out of any standing pool, and showed him through a magnifying-glass, in that single drop of water, dozens, perhaps hundreds, of living creatures so small that it is impossible to see them with the naked eye, each of them of some beautiful and wonderful shape, unlike anything which you ever saw or dreamed of, but each of them alive, each of them moving, feeding, breeding, after its kind, each fulfilling the nature which God has given to them, and told him, 'All the whole world, the air which you breathe, the leaves on the trees, the soil under your feet, ay, even often the food which you eat, and your own flesh and blood, are as full of wonderful things as that drop of water is. You fancy that all the life in the world is made up of the men and women in it, and the few beasts, and birds, and insects, which you see about you in the fields. But these living things which you do see are not a millionth part of the whole number of God's creatures; and not one smallest plant or tiniest insect dies, but what it passes into a new life, and becomes food for other creatures, even smaller than, though just as wonderful as itself. Every day fresh living creatures are being discovered, filling earth, and sea, and air, till men's brains are weary with counting them, and dizzy with watching their unspeakable beauty, and strangeness, and fitness for the work which God has given each of them to do.'

And then suppose I said to the child, 'God cares for each of these tiny living creatures. How do you know that He does not care for them as much as He does for you? God made them for His own pleasure, that He might rejoice in the work of His own hands. How do you know that He does not rejoice in them as much as in you? Those mighty worlds and suns above your head, which you call stars, how do you know that they are not as much more glorious and precious in God's sight than you are, as they are larger and more beautiful than you are? And mind! all these things, from the tiniest insects in the water-drop, to the most vast star or comet in the sky, all obey God. They have not fallen, as you have; they have not sinned, as you have; they have not broken the law, by which God intended them to live, as you have. The Bible tells you so; and the discoveries of learned men prove that the Bible is right, when it declares that they all continue to this day according to His ordinance; for all things serve Him; that sun, and moon, and stars, and light are praising Him; that fire and hail, snow and vapour, wind and storm, mountains and all hills, fruitful trees and all cedars, beasts and all cattle, worms and feathered fowl, are showing forth His glory day and night; because He has made them sure for ever and ever, each according to its kind, and given them a law which shall not be broken; for all His works praise Him, and show the glory of His kingdom, and the mightiness of His power, that His power, His glory, and the mightiness of His kingdom might be known unto the children of men.

And you!—They keep God's ordinance, and you have broken it; they fulfil God's word, you fulfil your own fancies. They have a law which shall not be broken, you break God's law daily. Are not they better than you? Is not, not merely sun and stars, but even the meanest gnat which hums in the air, better than man, more worthy of God's love than man? For man has sinned, and they have not.'

Do you not think that I should sadden, and terrify the child, and make him ready to cry out, 'Whither shall I flee from the wrath of this great Almighty God; who has made this wondrous heaven and earth, and all of it obeys Him, except me—I a rebel against Him who made and rules all this?'

My friends, I only say, suppose that I spoke thus to your children. For God forbid that I should speak thus to any human being, without having first taught him the Lord's Prayer, without first having taught him to say, 'I believe in Jesus Christ, Very God of Very God, who was born of the Virgin Mary, and took man's nature on Him;' without having taught him to say, 'Our Father which art in heaven, Thine is the kingdom, and the power, and the glory, for ever and ever, Amen.' So it is, and so let it be: for so it is well, and so I am safe, sinner and rebel though I be.

I would not say it, unless I had taught him this; for then I should be speaking the Devil's words, and doing the Devil's work: for these are the thoughts of which he always takes advantage, whenever he finds them in men's hearts; because he is the enemy who hates men, and the avenger who punishes them for their bad thoughts, by leading them on into dark and fearful deeds; because he is the Devil, the Slanderer, as his name means, and slanders God to men, and tries always to make them believe that God does not care for men, and grudges them blessings; in order that he may make men dread God, and shrink from Him into their own pride, or their own carnal lusts and fancies.

These are the thoughts of which the Devil took advantage in the heathen in old times, and tempted them to forget God—God, who had not left Himself without a witness, in that He gave them rain and fruitful seasons, filling their hearts with food and gladness—God, whose unseen glory, even His eternal power and Godhead, may be clearly seen from the creation of the world, being understood from the things which are made—God, in whom, as St. Paul told the heathen, they lived and moved, and had their being, and were the offspring of God. This—that man is the offspring of God, and has a Father in heaven—is the great truth which the Devil has been trying to hide from men in every age, and by a hundred different devices. By making them forget this, he tempted them to worship the creature instead of the Creator; to pray to sun and moon and stars, to send them fair weather, good crops, prosperous fortune: to look up to the heaven above them, and down to the earth beneath their feet, in slavish dread and anxiety: and pray to the sun, not to blast them to the seas, not to sweep them away; to the rivers and springs, not to let them perish from drought; to earthquakes, not to swallow them up; ay, even to try to appease those dark fierce powers, with whom they thought the great awful world was filled, by cruel sacrifices of human beings; so that they offered their sons and their daughters to devils, and burned their own children in the fire to Moloch, the cruel angry Fire King, whom they fancied was lord of the earthquakes and the burning mountains. So did the Canaanites of old, and so did the Jews after them; whensoever they had forgotten that God was their Father, who had bought them, and that the kingdom, and the power, and the glory, throughout heaven and earth, were His, then at once they began to be afraid of heaven and earth, and worshipped Baalim, and Astaroth, and the Host of Heaven, which were the sun and moon and stars, and Moloch the Fire King, and Thammuz the Lord of the Spring-time, and with forms of worship which showed plainly enough, either by their cruelty or their filthy profligacy, who was the author of them, and that man, when he forgets that heaven and earth belong to his Father, is in danger of becoming a slave to his own lowest lusts and passions.

And do not fancy, my friends, that because you and I are not likely to worship sun and moon and stars as the old heathen did, that therefore we cannot commit the same sin as they did.

My friends, I believe that we are in more danger of committing it in England just now than ever we were; that learned men especially are in danger of so doing, because they know so far more of the wonders and the vastness of God's creation than the heathens of old knew.

But you are not learned, you will say: you are plain people, who know nothing about these wonderful discoveries which men make by telescopes and magnifying-glasses, but use your own eyes in a plain way to get your daily bread, and you feel no such temptations. You believe, of course, that the kingdom and power and glory of all we see is God's.

Yes; but do you believe too that He whom people are too apt to call God, just because they have no other name to call Him, is your Father? That it is your Father's will which governs the weather, which makes the earth bear fruit and gladden the heart of man with good and fruitful seasons?

Alas, my friends, if we will open our eyes, see things in their true light, and call things by their true name, we shall see many a man in England now honouring the creature more than the Creator; trusting in the seasons and the soil more than he does in God, and so sinning in just the same way as the heathen of old.

When people say to themselves, 'I must get land, I must get money, by any means; honestly if I can, if not, dishonestly; for have it I must;' what are they doing then but denying that the kingdom, the power, and the glory of this earth belong to the Righteous God, and that He, and not the lying Devil, gives them to whomsoever He will?

When people say to themselves (as who does not at moments?) 'To be rich is to be safe; a man's life does consist in the abundance of what he possesses;' what are they doing but saying that man does not live by every word which proceeds out of the mouth of God, but by what he can get for himself and keep for himself? When they are fretful and anxious about their crops, when they even repine and complain of Providence, as I have known men do because they do not prosper as they wish, what are they doing but saying in their hearts, 'The weather and the seasons are the lords and masters of my good fortune, or bad fortune. I depend on them, and not on God, for comfort and for wealth, and my Heavenly Father does not know what I have need of?' When parents send their girls out to field-work, without any care about whom they talk with, to have their minds corrupted by hearing filthiness and seeing immodest behaviour, what are they doing but offering their daughters in sacrifice, not even to Moloch, but to Mammon; saying to themselves, 'My daughter's modesty, my daughter's virtue, is not of as much value as the paltry money which I can earn by leaving her alone to learn wickedness, instead of keeping watch over her, if she does work, that she may be none the worse for her day's labour.'

I might go on and give you a thousand instances more, but they all come alike to this; that whensoever you fancy that you cannot earn your daily bread without doing wrong yourself, or leaving your children to learn wrong, then you do not believe that the kingdom, the power, and the glory of this earth on which you work is your Heavenly Father's. For if you did, you would be certain that gains, large or small, got by breaking the least of His commandments, could never prosper you, but must bring a curse and a punishment with them; and you would be sure also, that because God is your Father, and this earth and all herein is His, that He would feed you with food sufficient for you, if you do but seek first His kingdom— that is, try to learn His laws; and seek first His righteousness—that is, strive and pray day by day to become righteous even as He is righteous.

Yes, my friends, this is one meaning, though only one, of St. John's words, 'This is the victory which overcometh the world, even our faith.' We all see the world full of pleasant things, for which we long; of necessary things, too, without which we should starve and die. And then the temptation comes to us to snatch at these things for ourselves by any means in our power, right or wrong; like the dumb animals who break out of their owners' field into the next, if they do but see better pasturage there, or fight and quarrel between themselves for food, each trying to get the most for himself and rob his neighbour. So live the beasts, and so you and I, and every human being shall be tempted to live, if we follow our natures, if we forget that we are God's children, in God's kingdom, under the laws of a Heavenly Father, who has shown forth His own love and justice, His own kingdom, and power, and glory, in the person of the Lord Jesus Christ. But if we remember that, if we remember daily that the kingdom, and power, and glory is our Father's, then we shall neither fear storms and blights, bad crops, or anything else which is of the earth earthly. We shall fear nothing of that kind, which can only kill the body, but only fear the evil Devil, lest, by making us distrust and disobey our Heavenly Father, he should, after he has killed, destroy both body and soul in hell. And as long as we fear him, as long as we renounce him, as long as we trust utterly in our Heavenly Father's love and justice, and in the love and justice of His dear Son, the Man Christ Jesus, to whom all power is given in heaven and earth—then out of the youngest child among us will God's praise be perfected; for the youngest child among us, by faith in God his Father, may look upon all heaven and earth, and say, 'Great, and wonderful, and awful as this earth and skies may be, I am more precious in the sight of God than sun, and moon, and stars; for they are things: but I am a person, a spirit, an immortal soul, made in the likeness of God, redeemed into the likeness of God, sanctified into the likeness of God. This great earth was here thousands and thousands of years before I was born, and it will be here perhaps millions and millions of years after I am dead; but it cannot harm me; it cannot kill me. When earth, and sun, and stars are past away, I shall live for ever; for I am the immortal child of an Immortal Father, the child of the everlasting God. These things He only made: but me He begot unto everlasting life, in Jesus Christ my Lord. I seem to depend on this earth for food, for clothing, for comfort, for life itself: and yet I do not do so in reality; for man doth not live by bread alone, but by every word which proceeds out of the mouth of God my Father. In Him I have eternal life: a life which this earth did not give, and cannot take away; a life which, by the mercy of my Father in heaven, I trust and hope to be living when sun and earth, stars and comets, are returned again to their dust, and blotted from the face of heaven. For the kingdom, the glory, and the power of this world, and all other worlds, past, present, and to come, belong to Him who spared not His only-begotten Son, but freely gave Him for us, and will with Him freely give us all things.'

And thus, my friends, may God's praise be perfected out of the mouth of any Christian child, when He declares that God put man a little lower than the angels only to crown him with the glory and worship of having the only-begotten Son of God take man's nature upon Him, and walk this earth as a man, and live, and die, and rise again as a man, that so He might raise fallen man again to the glory and honour which God appointed for men from the beginning, when He said, Let us make man in our image, after our likeness: and let them have dominion over the fish of the sea and the fowl of the air, and the beast of the earth; and be fruitful and multiply, and replenish the earth and subdue it.

SERMON XI

AHAB AND NABOTH

And Ahab spake unto Naboth, saying, Give me thy
vineyard, that I may have it for a garden of herbs,
because it is near unto my house: and I will give thee
for it a better vineyard than it; or, if it seem good to
thee, I will give thee the worth of it in money. And
Naboth said unto Ahab, The Lord forbid it me, that I
should give the inheritance of my fathers unto thee.

1 Kings xxi. 2, 3.

You heard to-day read for the first lesson, the story of Naboth and King Ahab. Most of you know it well. Naboth's vineyard has passed into a proverb for something which we covet.

It is good that it should be so. We cannot know our Bible too well; we cannot have Bible words and Bible thoughts too much worked into our ways of talking and thinking about everyday matters. As far as I can see, the best days of England, the best days of every Christian country of which I ever read, have been days when men were not ashamed of their Bibles; when they were ready to live by their Bibles; to ask advice of their Bibles about buying and selling, about making war and peace, about all the business of life; and were not ashamed to quote texts of Scripture in the parliament, and in the market, and in the battle-field, as God's law, God's rule, God's word about the matter in hand, which was, therefore, sure to be the right word and the right rule. People are grown ashamed of doing so now-a-days; but that does not alter the matter one jot. We may deny God, but He cannot deny Himself. His laws are everlasting, and He is ruling and judging us by them now, all day long, just as much as He ruled and judged those Jews by them of old. The God of Abraham is our God; the God of Moses is our God; the God of Ahab and Naboth is our God; neither He nor His government are altered in the least since their time, and they never will alter for ever, and ever, and ever; and if we do not choose to believe that now in this life, we shall be made to believe it by some very ugly and painful schooling in the life to come.

What laws of God, now, can we learn from this story?

First, we may learn what a sacred thing property is. That a man's possessions (if they be justly come by) belong to him, in the sight of God as well as in the sight of man, and that God will uphold and avenge the man's right.

Naboth, you see, stands simply on his right to his own property. 'The Lord forbid it me, that I should give the inheritance of my fathers unto thee.' I do not think that he meant that God had actually forbidden him: it seems to have been only some sort of oath which he used. He may certainly have had reasons for thinking it wrong to part with his lands; hurtful, perhaps, to his family after him. Yet, as Ahab had promised him a better vineyard for it, or its worth in money, I cannot help thinking that Naboth's reason was the one which shows on the face of his words. It was the inheritance of his fathers, this vineyard. They had all worked in it, generation after generation; perhaps, according to the Jewish custom, they were buried somewhere in it; at least, it had been theirs and now was his; he had worked in it, and played in it—perhaps since he was a child—and he loved it; it was part and parcel of his father's house to him, a sacred spot.

And so it should be. It is a holy feeling which makes a man cling to the bit of land which he has inherited from his parents, even to the cottage, though it be only a hired one, where he has lived for many a year, and where he has planted and tilled, perhaps with some that he loved, who are now dead and gone, or grown up and gone out into the world, till the little old cottage-garden is full of remembrances to him of past joys and past sorrows. The feeling which makes a man cling to his home and to his own land is a good feeling, and breeds good in the man. It makes him respect himself; it keeps him from being reckless and unsettled. It is a feeling which should not be broken through. It is seldom pleasant to see land change hands; it is seldom pleasant to see people turned out of their cottages. It must often be so, but let it be as seldom as possible. One likes to see a family take root in a place, and grow and thrive there, one generation after another; and you will find, my friends, that families do take root and thrive in a place just in proportion as they fear God and do righteousness. The Psalms tell you, again and again, that the way to abide in the land, and prosper in it, is to trust in the Lord and be doing good; and that the wicked are soon rooted out, and their names perish out of the land. One sees that come true daily.

But to return to Naboth. He loved his own land, and therefore he had a right to keep it. We may say it was but a fancy of his, if he could have a better vineyard, or the worth of it in money. Remember, at least, that God respected that fancy of his, and justified it, and avenged it. When (after Naboth's death) Elijah accused Ahab, in God's name, he put two counts into the indictment; for Ahab had committed two sins. 'Hast thou killed, and also taken possession?' Killing was one sin; taking possession was another.

And so Ahab learnt two weighty and bitter lessons. He learnt that God's Law stands for ever, though man's law be broken or be forgotten by disuse. For you must understand, that these Jews were a free people, even as we are. They were not like the nations round about them, or as the Russians are now—slaves to their king, and holding their property only at his will. The law of Moses had made them a free people, who held their property each man from God, by God's Law, which had said, 'Thou shalt not steal. Thou shalt not covet. Cursed is he who removes his neighbour's landmark.' And their kings were bound to govern by Moses' law, just as our kings and rulers are bound to govern by the old constitutions of England, and to do equal justice by rich and poor. But the wicked kings of Israel were trying to break through that law, and make themselves tyrants and despots, such as the Czar of Russia is now. First, Jeroboam began by trying to wean his people from Moses' law, by preventing their going up to worship at Jerusalem, and making them worship instead the golden calves at Dan and at Bethel. For he knew that if he could make idolaters of them, he should soon make slaves of them; and he succeeded; and the kingdom of Israel grew more miserable year by year; and now Ahab, his wicked successor, was breaking down the laws of property and wrongfully taking away his subjects' lands. Perhaps he said in his heart, 'I am king; there is no law stronger than I. I have a right to do what I like.' If he did so, he found that he was mistaken. He found that though he forgot Moses' law, God had not; that the law stood there still, because it was founded on eternal justice, which proceeds for ever out of the mouth of God; and by the Law, which he had chosen to forget, he was judged; by the Law of God, which deals equal justice to rich and poor, which is, like God Himself, no acceptor of persons; but says, 'Thou shalt not covet,' to the king upon his throne as sternly as to the beggar on the dunghill.

And that Law stands still, my friends, doubt it not. Thanks to the wisdom and justice of our forefathers who built the laws of England on those old Ten Commandments, which hang for a sign thereof in every church to this day. Thanks to them, I say, and to God, the root of the law of England is, equal justice between man and man, be he high or low; and it is a thing to bless God for every day of our lives, that here the poor man's little is as safe as the rich man's wealth: but there is many a sin of oppression, many a sin of covetousness, my friends, which no law of man can touch. Make laws as artfully as you will, bad men can always slip through them, and escape the spirit of them, while they obey the letter: and I suppose it will be so to the world's end; and that, let the laws be as perfect as they may, if any man wishes to cheat or oppress his neighbour, he will surely be able to work his wicked will in some way or other. Well then, my friends, if man's law is weak, God's is not;—if man's law has flaws and gaps in it, through which covetousness can creep, God's has none;—even if (which God forbid) man's law died out, and sinners were left to sin without fear of punishment, still God's Law stands sure, and the eye of the living God slumbers not, and the hand of the living God never grows weary, and out of the everlasting heaven His voice is saying, day and night, for ever, 'I endure for ever. I sit on the throne judging right; a sceptre of righteousness is the sceptre of My kingdom. I judge the world in justice, and minister true judgment unto the people. I also will be a refuge for the oppressed, even a refuge in due time of trouble.'

O hear those words, my friends! hear and obey, if you love life, and wish to see good days; and never, never say a thing is right, simply because the law cannot punish you for it. Never say in your hearts when you are tempted to be hard, cruel, covetous, over-reaching, 'What harm? I break no law by it.' There is a law, whether you see it or not; you break a law, whether you confess it or not; a law which is as a wall of iron clothed with thunder, though man's law be but a flimsy net of thread; and that law, and not any Acts of Parliament, shall judge you in the day when the secrets of all hearts shall be disclosed, and every man shall receive the due reward of the deeds done in the body, not according as they were allowed or not by the Statute Book, but according as they were good or evil.

Another lesson we may learn from this story: that if we give way to our passions, we give way to the Devil also. Ahab gave way to his passion; he knew that he was wrong; for when Naboth refused to sell him the vineyard, he did not dare openly to rob him of it; he went to his house heavy of heart, and fretted, like a spoilt child, because he could not get what he wanted. It was but a little thing, and he might have been content to go without it. He was king of all Israel, and what was one small vineyard more or less to him? But prosperity had spoilt him; he must needs have every toy on which he set his heart, and he was weak enough to fret that he could not get more, when he had too much already. But he knew that he could not get it; that, king as he was, Naboth's property was his own, and that God's everlasting Law stood between him and the thing he coveted. Well for him if he had been contented with fretting. But, my friends—and be you rich or poor, take heed to my words—whenever any man gives way to selfishness, and self-seeking, to a proud, covetous, envious, peevish temper, the Devil is sure to glide up and whisper in his ear thoughts which will make him worse—worse, ay, than he ever dreamt of being. First comes the flesh, and then the Devil; and if the flesh opens the door of the heart, the Devil steps in quickly enough. First comes the flesh: fleshly, carnal pride at being thwarted; fleshly, carnal longing for a thing, which longs all the more for it because one cannot have it; fleshly, carnal peevishness and ill-temper, at not having just the pleasant thing one happens to like. That is a state of mind which is a bird-call for all the devils; and when they see a man in that temper, they flock to him, I believe, as crows do to carrion. It is astonishing, humbling, awful, my friends, what horrible thoughts will cross one's mind if once one gives way to that selfish, proud, angry, longing temper; thoughts of which we are ashamed the next moment; temptations to sin at which we shudder, they seem so unlike ourselves, not parts of ourselves at all. When the dark fit is past, one can hardly believe that such wicked thoughts ever crossed one's mind. I don't think that they are part of ourselves; I believe them to be the whispers of the Devil himself; and when they pass away, I believe that it is the Lord Jesus Christ who drives them away. But if any man gives way to them, determines to keep his sullenness, and so gives place to the Devil; then those thoughts do not pass; they take hold of a man, possess him, as the Bible calls it, and make him in his madness do things which—alas! who has not done things in his day, of which he has repented all his life after?—things for which he would gladly cut off his right hand for the sake of being able to say, 'I never did that?' But the thing is done—done to all eternity: he has given place to the Devil, and the Devil has made him do in five minutes work which he could not undo in five thousand years; and all that is left is, when he comes to himself, to cast himself on God's boundless mercy, and Christ's boundless atonement, and cry, 'My sins are like scarlet, Thou alone canst make them whiter than snow: my sin is ever before me; only let it not be ever before Thee, O God! Punish me, if thou seest fit; but oh forgive, for there is mercy with Thee, and infinite redemption!' And, thanks be to God's great love, he will not cry in vain. Yet, oh, my friends, do not give place to the Devil, unless you wish, forgiven or not, to repent of it to the latest day you live.

And this was Ahab's fate. He knew, I say, that he was wrong; he knew that Naboth's property was his own, and dare not openly rob him of it; and he went to his house, heavy of heart, and refused to eat; and while he was in such a temper as that, the Devil lost no time in sending an evil spirit to him. It was a woman whom he sent, Jezebel, Ahab's own wife: but she was, as far as we can see, a woman of a devilish spirit, cruel, proud, profligate, and unjust, as well as a worshipper of the filthy idols of the Canaanites. Ahab's first sin was in having married this wicked heathen woman: now his sin punished itself; she tempted him through his pride and self-conceit; she taunted him into sin: 'Dost thou now govern the kingdom of Israel? I will give thee the vineyard of Naboth.' You all remember how she did so; by falsely accusing Naboth of blasphemy. Ahab seems to have taken no part in Naboth's murder. Perhaps he was afraid; but he was a weak man, and Jezebel was a strong and fierce spirit, and ruled him, and led him in this matter, as she did in making him worship idols with her; and he was content to be led. He was content to let others do the wickedness he had not courage to carry out himself. He forgot that, as is well said, 'He who does a thing by another, does it by himself;' that if you let others sin for you, you sin for yourself. Would to God, my friends, that we would all remember this! How often people wink at wrong-doing in those with whom they have dealings, in those whom they employ, in their servants, in their children, because it is convenient to them. They shut their eyes, and their hearts too, and say to themselves, 'At all events, it is his doing and not mine; and it is his concern; I am not answerable for other people's sins. I would not do such a thing myself, certainly; but as it is done, I may as well make the best of it. If I gain by it, I need not be so very sharp in looking into the matter.' And so you see men who really wish to be honest and kindly themselves, making no scruple of profiting by other people's dishonesty and cruelty. Now the law punishes the receiver of stolen goods almost as severely as the thief himself: but there are many receivers of stolen goods, my friends, whom the law cannot touch. The world, at times, seems to me to be full of them; for every one, my friends, who hushes up a cruel or a dishonest matter, because he himself is a gainer by it, he is no better than the receiver of stolen goods, and he will find in the day of the Lord, that the sin will lie at his door, as Jezebel's sin lay at Ahab's. There was no need for Ahab to say, 'Jezebel did it, and not I.' The prophet did not even give him time to excuse himself: 'Thus saith the Lord, Hast thou killed, and also taken possession?' By taking possession of Naboth's vineyard, and so profiting by his murder, he made himself partaker in that murder, and had to hear the terrible sentence, 'In the place where dogs licked the blood of Naboth, dogs shall lick thy blood, even thine.'

Oh, my friends, whatsoever you do, keep clean hands and a

pure heart. If you touch pitch, it will surely stick to you. Let no gain tempt you to be partaker of others men's sins; never fancy that, because men cannot lay the blame on the right person, God cannot. God will surely lay the burden on the man who helped to make the burden; God will surely require part payment from the man who profited by the bargain; so keep yourselves clear of other men's sins, that you may be clear also of their condemnation.

So Ahab had committed a horrible and great sin, and had received sentence for it, and now, as I said before, there was nothing to be done but to repent; and he did so, after his fashion.

Ahab, it seems, was not an utterly bad man; he was a weak man, fond of his own pleasure, a slave to his own passions, and easily led, sometimes to good, but generally to evil. And God did not execute full vengeance on him: his repentance was a poor one enough; but such as it was, the good and merciful God gave him credit for it as far as it went, and promised him that the worst part of his sentence, the ruin of his family, should not come in his time. But still the sentence against him stood, and was fulfilled. Not long after, as we read in the second lesson, he was killed in battle, and that not bravely and with honour (for if he had been, that would have been but a slight punishment, my friends), but shamefully by a chance shot, after he had disguised himself, in the cowardice of his guilty conscience, and tried to throw all the danger on his ally, good King Jehoshaphat of Judah; 'and they washed his chariot in the pool of Samaria, and the dogs licked up his blood, according to the word of the Lord, which he spake by Elijah the prophet.'

So ends one of the most clear and terrible stories in the whole Bible, of God's impartial justice. May God give us all grace to lay it to heart! We are all tempted, as Ahab was; rich or poor, our temptation is alike to give place to the Devil, and let him lead us into dark and deep sin, by giving way to our own fancies, longings, pride, and temper. We are all tempted, as Ahab was, to over-reach our neighbours in some way; I do not mean always in cheating them, but in being unfair to them, in caring more for ourselves than for them; thinking of ourselves first, and of them last; trying to make ourselves comfortable, or to feed our own pride, at their expense. Oh, my friends, whenever we are tempted to be selfish and grasping, be sure that we are opening a door to the very Devil of hell himself, though he may look so smooth, and gentle, and respectable, that perhaps we shall not know him when he comes to us, and shall take his counsels for the counsel of an angel of light. But be sure that if it is selfishness which has opened the door of our heart, not God, but the Devil, will come in, let him disguise himself as cunningly as he will; and our only hope is to flee to Him in whom there was no selfishness, the Lord Jesus Christ, who came not to do His own will, but His Father's; not to glorify Himself, but His Father; not to save His own life, but to sacrifice it freely, for us, His selfish, weak, greedy, wandering sheep. Pray to Him to give you His Spirit, that glorious spirit of love, and duty, and self-sacrifice, by which all the good deeds on earth are done; which teaches a man not to care about himself, but about others; to help others, to feel for others, to rejoice in their happiness, to grieve over their sorrows, to give to them, rather than take from them—in one word, The Holy Spirit of God, which may He pour out on you, and me, and all mankind, that we may live justly and lovingly, as children of one just and loving Father in heaven.

THE LIGHT OF GOD

[Preached for the Chelsea National Schools]

*All things which are reproved are made manifest by
the light: for whatsoever is made manifest is light.*

Ephesians v. 13.

This is a noble text, a royal text; one of those texts which forbid
us to clip and cramp Scripture to suit any narrow notions of our
own; which open before us boundless vistas of God's love, of human
knowledge, of the future of mankind. There are many such texts,
many more than we fancy; but this is one which is especially
valuable at the present time; one especially fit for a sermon on
education; for it is, as it were, the scriptural charter of the advocate
of education. It enables him boldly to say, 'There is nothing I will
refuse to teach; there is nothing which man shall forbid me to teach;
there is nothing which God has made in heaven or earth about
which I will not tell the truth boldly to the young.'

For light comes from God. God is light, and in Him is no
darkness at all. And therefore He wishes to give light to His
children. He willeth not that the least of them should be kept in
darkness about any matter. Darkness is of the Devil; and he who
keeps any human soul in darkness, let his pretences be as reverent
and as religious as they may, is doing the Devil's work. Nothing,
then, which God has made will we conceal from the young.

True, there are errors of which we will not speak to the young;
but they are not made by God: they are the works of darkness. Our
duty is to teach the young what God has made, what He has done,
what He has ordained; to make them freely partakers of whatsoever
light God has given us. Then, by means of that light, they will be
able to reprove the works of darkness.

For whatsoever is made manifest is light. Our version says;
'Whatsoever makes manifest is light.' That is true, a noble truth;
but I should not be honest, if I did not confess that that is not what
St. Paul says here. He says, 'That which is made manifest is light.'

On this the best commentators and scholars agree. Our old translators have made a mistake, though in grammar only, and have substituted one great truth for another equally great.

'Whatsoever is made manifest is light.' We should have expected this, if we are really Christians. If we have faith in God; if we believe that God is worthy of our faith—a God whom we can trust; in whom is neither caprice, deceit, nor darkness, but pure and perfect light;—if we believe that we are His children, and that He wishes us to be, like Himself, full of light, knowing what we are and what the world is, because we know who God is;—if we believe that He sent His Son into the world to reveal Him, to unveil Him, to draw aside the veil which dark superstition and ignorance had spread between man and God, and to show us the glory of God;—if we believe this, then we shall be ready to expect that whatsoever is made manifest would be light; for if God be light, all that He has made must be light also. Like must beget like, and therefore light must beget light, good beget good, love beget love; and therefore we ought to expect that as true and sound knowledge increases, our views of God will be more full of light.

Yes, my friends; under the influence of true science God will be no longer looked upon, as He was in those superstitions which we well call dark, as a proud, angry, capricious being, as a stern taskmaster, as one far removed from the sympathy of men: but as one of whom we may cheerfully say, Thy name be hallowed, for Thy name is Father; Thy kingdom come, for it is a Father's kingdom; Thy will be done, for it is a Father's will; and in doing Thy will alone men claim their true dignity of being the sons of God.

Our views of our fellow-men will be more cheerful also; more full of sympathy, comprehension, charity, hope; in one word, more full of light. If it be true (and it is true) that God loves all, then we should expect to find in all something worthy of our love. If it be true that God willeth that none should perish, we should expect to find in each man something which ought not to perish. If it be true that God stooped from heaven, yea stoops from heaven eternally, to seek and to save that which is lost, then we should have good hope that our efforts to seek to save that which is lost will not be in vain. We shall have hope in every good work we undertake, for we shall know that in it we are fellow-workers with God.

Our notions of the world—of God's whole universe, will become full of light likewise. Do we believe that this earth was made by Jesus Christ?—by Him who was full of grace and truth? Do we believe our Bibles, when they tell us, that He hath given all created things a law which cannot be broken; that they continue as at the beginning, for all things serve Him? Do we believe this? Then we must look on this earth, yea on the whole universe of God, as, like its Master, full of grace and truth; not as old monks and hermits fancied it, a dark, deceiving, evil earth, filled with snares and temptations; a world from which a man ought to hide himself in the wilderness, and find his own safety in ignorance. Not thus, but as the old Hebrews thought of it, as a glorious and a divine universe, in which the Spirit of God, the Lord and Giver of life, creates eternal melody, bringing for ever life out of death, light out of darkness, letting his breath go forth that new generations may be made, and herein renew the face of the earth.

And experience teaches us that this has been the case; that for near one thousand eight hundred years there has been a steady progress in the mind of the Christian race, and that this progress has been in the direction of light.

Has it not been so in our notions of God? What has the history of theology been for near one thousand eight hundred years? Has it not been a gradual justification of God, a gradual vindication of His character from those dark and horrid notions of the Deity which were borrowed from the Pagans, and from the Jewish Rabbis? a gradual return to the perfect good news of a good God, which was preached by St. John and by St. Paul?—In one word, a gradual manifestation of God; and a gradual discovery that when God is manifested, behold, God is light, and in Him is no darkness at all?

That progress, alas! is not yet perfect. We still see through a glass darkly, and we are still too apt to impute to God Himself the darkness of those very hearts of ours in which He is so dimly mirrored. And there are men still, even in Protestant England, who love darkness rather than light, and teach men that God is dark, and in Him are only scattered spots of light, and those visible only to a favoured few; men who, whether from ignorance, or covetousness, or lust of power, preach such a deity as the old Pharisees worshipped, when they crucified the Lord of Glory, and offer to deliver men, forsooth, out of the hands of this dreadful phantom of their own dark imaginations.

Let them be. Let the dead bury their dead, and let us follow Christ. Believe indeed that He is the likeness of God's glory, and the express image of God's person, and you will be safe from the dark dreams with which they ensnare diseased and superstitious consciences. Let them be. Light is stronger than darkness; Love stronger than cruelty. Perfect God stronger than fallen man; and the day shall come when all shall be light in the Lord; when all mankind shall know God, from the least unto the greatest, and lifting up free foreheads to Him who made them, and redeemed them by His Son, shall in spirit and in truth, worship The Father.

Does not experience again show us that in the case of our fellow-men, whatsoever is made manifest, is light?

How easy it was, a thousand years ago—a hundred years ago even, to have dark thoughts about our fellow-men, simply because we did not know them! Easy it was, while the nations were kept apart by war, even by mere difficulty of travelling, for Christians to curse Jews, Turks, Infidels, and Heretics, and believe that God willed their eternal perdition, even though the glorious collect for Good Friday gave their inhumanity the lie. Easy to persecute those to whose opinions we could not, or would not, take the trouble to give a fair hearing. Easy to condemn the negro to perpetual slavery, when we knew nothing of him but his black face; or to hang by hundreds the ragged street-boys, while we disdained to inquire into the circumstances which had degraded them; or to treat madmen as wild beasts, instead of taming them by wise and gentle sympathy.

But with a closer knowledge of our fellow-creatures has come toleration, pity, sympathy. And as that sympathy has been freely obeyed, it has justified itself more and more. The more we have tried to help our fellow-men, the more easy we have found it to help them. The more we have trusted them, the more trustworthy we have found them. The more we have treated them as human beings, the more humanity we have found in them. And thus man, in proportion as he becomes manifest to man, is seen, in spite of all defects and sins, to be hallowed with a light from God who made him.

And if it has been thus, in the case of God and of humanity, has it not been equally so in the case of the physical world? Where are now all those unnatural superstitions—the monkish contempt for marriage and social life, the ghosts and devils; the astrology, the magic, and other dreams of which I will not speak here, which made this world, in the eyes of our forefathers, a doleful and dreadful puzzle; and which made man the sport of arbitrary powers, of cruel beings, who could torment and destroy us, but over whom we could have no righteous power in return? Where are all those dark dreams gone which maddened our forefathers into witch-hunting panics, and which on the Continent created a priestly science of witch-finding and witch-destroying, the literature whereof (and it is a large one) presents perhaps the most hideous instance known of human cruelty, cowardice, and cunning? Where, I ask, are those dreams now? So utterly vanished, that very few people in this church know what a great part they played in the thoughts of our forefathers; how ghosts, devils, witches, magic, and astrology, filled the minds, not only of the ignorant, but of the most learned, for centuries.

And now, behold, nature being made manifest, is light. Science has taught men to admire where they used to dread; to rule where they used to obey; to employ for harmless uses what they were once afraid to touch; and, where they once saw only fiends, to see the orderly and beneficent laws of the all-good and almighty God. Everywhere, as the work of nature is unfolded to our eyes, we see beauty, order, mutual use, the offspring of perfect Love as well as perfect Wisdom. Everywhere we are finding means to employ the secret forces of nature for our own benefit, or to ward off physical evils which seemed to our forefathers as inevitable, supernatural; and even the pestilence, instead of being, as was once fancied, the capricious and miraculous infliction of some demon—the pestilence itself is found to be an orderly result of the same laws by which the sun shines and the herb grows; a product of nature; and therefore subject to man, to be prevented and extirpated by him, if he will.

Yes, my friends, let us teach these things to our children, to all children. Let us tell them to go to the Light, and see their Heavenly Father's works manifested, and know that they are, as He is, Light. I say, let us teach our children freely and boldly to know these things, and grow up in the light of them. Let us leave those to sneer at the triumphs of modern science, who trade upon the ignorance and the cowardice of mankind, and who say, 'Provided you make a child religious, what matter if he does fancy the sun goes round the earth? Why occupy his head, perhaps disturb his simple faith, by giving him a smattering of secular science?'

Specious enough is that argument: but shortsighted more than enough. It is of a piece with the wisdom which shrinks from telling children that God is love, lest they should not be sufficiently afraid of Him; which forbids their young hearts to expand freely towards their fellow-creatures: which puts into their mouths the watchwords of sects and parties, and thinks to keep them purer Christians by making them Pharisees from the cradle.

My friends, we may try to train up children as Pharisees: but we shall discover, after twenty years of mistaken labour, that we have only made them Sadducees. The path to infidelity in manhood is superstition in youth. You may tell the child never to mind whether the sun moves round the earth or not: but the day will come when he will mind in spite of you; and if he then finds that you have deceived him, that you have even left him in wilful ignorance, all your moral influence over him is gone, and all your religious lessons probably gone also. So true is it, that lies are by their very nature self-destructive. For all truth is of God; and no lie is of the truth, and therefore no lie can possibly help God or God's work in any human soul. For as the child ceases to respect his teachers he ceases to respect what they believe. His innate instinct of truth and honour, his innate longing to believe, to look up to some one better than himself, have been shocked and shaken once and for all; and it may require long years, and sad years, to bring him back to the faith of his childhood. Again I say it, we must not fear to tell the children the whole truth; in these days above all others which the world has yet seen. You cannot prevent their finding out the truth: then for our own sake, let us, their authorized teachers, be the first to tell it them. Let them in after life connect the thought of their clergyman, their schoolmaster, their church, with their first lessons in the free and right use of their God-given faculties, with their first glimpses into the boundless mysteries of art and science. Let them learn from us to regard all their powers as their Heavenly Father's gift; all art, all science, all discoveries, as their Heavenly Father's revelation to men. Let them learn from us not to shrink from the light, not to peep at it by stealth, but to claim it as their birthright; to welcome it, to live and grow in it to the full stature of men—rational, free, Christian English men. This, I believe, must be the method of a truly Protestant education.

I said Protestant—I say it again. What is the watchword of Protestantism? It is this. That no lie is of the truth. There are those who complain of us English that we attach too high a value to truth. They say that falsehood is an evil: but not so great a one as we fancy. We accept the imputation. We answer boldly that there can be no greater evil than falsehood, no greater blessing than truth; and that by God's help we will teach the same to our children, and to our children's children. Free inquiry, religious as well as civil liberty— this is the spirit of Protestantism. This our fathers have bequeathed to us; this we will bequeath to our children;—to know that all truth is of God, that no lie is of the truth. Our enemies may call us heretics, unbelievers, rebellious, political squabblers. They may say in scorn, You Protestants know not whither you are going; you have broken yourselves off from the old Catholic tree, and now, in the wild exercise of your own private judgment, you are losing all that standard of doctrine, all unity of belief. Our answer will be—It is not so: but even if it were so—even if we did not know whither we were going—we should go forward still. For though we know not, God knows. We have committed ourselves to God, the living God; and He has led us; and we believe that He will lead us. He has taught us; and we believe that He will teach us still. He has prospered us, and we believe that He will prosper us still: and therefore we will train up our children after us to go on the path which has brought us hither, freely to use their minds, boldly to prove all things, and hold fast that which is good; manfully to go forward, following Truth whithersoever she may lead them; trusting in God, the Father of Lights, asking Him for wisdom, who giveth to all liberally, and upbraideth not; and it shall be given them.

I have been asked to preach this day for the National Schools of this parish. I do so willingly, because I believe that in them this course of education is pursued, that conjoined with a sound teaching in the principles of our Protestant church, and a wholesome and kindly moral training, there is free and full secular instruction as far as the ages of the children will allow. Were it not the case, I could not plead for these schools; above all at this time, when the battle between ancient superstition and modern enlightenment in this land seems fast coming to a crisis and a death struggle. I could not ask you to help any school on earth in which I had not fair proof that the teachers taught, on physical and human as well as on moral subjects, the truth, the whole truth, and nothing but the truth, so help them God.

SERMON XIII

PROVIDENCE

*Be not anxious, saying, What shall we eat? or, what
shall we drink, or wherewithal shall we be clothed?
(for after all these things do the heathen seek:) for
your Heavenly Father knoweth that ye have need of
all these things. But seek ye first the kingdom of God
and His righteousness, and all these things shall be
added unto you.*

Matthew vi. 31, 32, 33.

We must first consider carefully what this text really means;
what 'taking no thought for the morrow' really is. Now, it cannot
mean that we are to be altogether careless and imprudent; for all
Scripture, and especially Solomon's Proverbs, give us the very
opposite advice, and one part of God's Word cannot contradict the
other. The whole of Solomon's Proverbs is made up of lessons in
prudence and foresight; and surely our Lord did not come to do
away with Solomon's Proverbs, but to fulfil them. And more,
Solomon declares again and again, that prudence and foresight are
the gifts of God; and God's gifts are surely meant to be used. Isaiah,
too, tells us that the common work of the farm, tilling the ground,
sowing, and reaping, were taught to men by God; and says of the
ploughman, that 'His God doth instruct him to discretion and doth
teach him.' Neither can God mean us to sit idle with folded hands
waiting to be fed by miracles. Would He have given to man reason,
and skill, and the power of bettering his mortal condition by ten
thousand instructions if He had not meant him to use those gifts?
We find that, at the beginning, Adam is put into the garden, not to
sit idle in it, nor to feed merely on the fruits which fall from the
trees, as the dumb animals do, but to dress it, and to keep it; to use
his own reason to improve his own condition, and the land on which
God had placed him. Was not the very first command given to man
to replenish the earth and subdue it? And do we not find in the very
end of Scripture the Apostles working with their own hands for their
daily bread?

But what use of many words? It is absurd to believe anything else; absurd to believe that man was meant to live like the butterfly, flitting without care from flower to flower, and, like the butterfly, die helpless at the first shower or the first winter's frost. Whatever the text means, it cannot mean that.

And it does not mean that. I suppose, that three hundred years ago (when the Bible was translated out of the Greek tongue, in which the Apostles wrote, into English), 'taking thought' meant something different from what it does now: but the plain meaning of the text, if it be put into such English as we talk now, is, 'Do not fret about the morrow. Be not anxious about the morrow.' There is no doubt at all, as any scholar can tell you, that that is the plain meaning of the word in our modern English, and that our Lord is not telling us to be imprudent or idle, but not to be anxious and fretful about the morrow.

And more, I think if we look carefully at these words, we shall find that they tell us the very reason why we are to work, and to look forward, and to believe that God will bless our labour.

And what is this reason? It is this, that we have a Father in heaven; not a mere Maker, not a mere Master, but a Father. All turns on that one Gospel of all Gospels, your Father in heaven. For our Lord seems to me to say, 'Be not anxious for your life, what ye shall eat, or drink, or wear. Is not the life more than meat? Has not your Heavenly Father given you a higher life than the mere life which must be kept up by food, which He has given to the animals? He has made you reasonable souls; He has given to you wisdom from His own wisdom, and a share of the Light which lights every man who comes into the world, the Light of Christ His Son; He has created you in His own likeness, that like Him you may make things, be makers and inventors, each in his place and calling, each according to his talents and powers, even as your Heavenly Father, the Maker and Creator of all things. And if He has given you all these wonderful powers of mind and soul, surely He has given you the less blessing, the mere power to earn your own food? If He has made you so much wiser than the beasts, surely He has made you as wise as the beasts.' 'And is not the body more than raiment?' Has He not given you bodies which can speak, write, build, work, plant, in a thousand cunning and wonderful ways; bodies which can do a thousand nobler things than merely keep themselves warm, as the beasts do? Then be sure, if He has given you the greater power, He has given you the less also. And as for fine clothes and rich ornaments, 'Is not the body more than raiment?' Is not your body a far more beautiful and nobler thing than all the gay clothes with which you can bedizen it? If your bodies be fair, strong, healthy, useful, it matters little what clothes you put upon them. Why will you not have faith in your Heavenly Father? Why will you not have faith in the great honour which He put on you when He said at first, 'Let us make man in our image, after our likeness, and let him have dominion over all things on the earth'? Be sure, that God would not have made man, and given him all these powers, and sent him upon this earth, unless this earth had been a right good and fit place for him. Be sure that if you obey the laws of this earth where God has put you, you will never need to be anxious or fret; but you will prosper right well, you and your children after you. For 'Consider the fowls of the air, they neither sow, nor reap, and gather into barns, and yet your Heavenly Father feeds them; and are ye not much better than they?' Surely you are, for you can sow, and reap, and gather into barns. And if God makes the earth work so well that it feeds the fowls who cannot help themselves, how much more will the earth feed you who can help yourselves, because God has given you understanding and prudence? But as for anxiety, fretting, repining, complaining to God, 'Why hast Thou made me thus?' what use in that? 'Which of you by taking thought can add one cubit to his stature?' Will all the fretting and anxiety in the world make you one foot or one inch taller than you are? Will it make you stronger, wiser, more able to help yourself? You are what you are: you can do what God has given you power to do. Trust Him that He has made you strong enough and wise enough to earn your daily bread, and to prosper right well, if you will, upon this earth which He has made. And why be anxious about clothing? 'Consider the lilies of the field, how they grow; they toil not, neither do they spin; and yet Solomon in all his glory was not arrayed like one of these.' But man can toil, man can spin; your Heavenly Father has given to man the power of providing clothes for himself, and not for himself only, but for others; so that while the man who tills the soil feeds the man who spins and weaves, the man who spins and weaves shall clothe the man who tills the soil; and the town shall work for the country, while the country feeds the town; and every man, if he does but labour where God has put him, shall produce comforts for human beings whom he never saw, who live perhaps in foreign lands across the sea. For the Heavenly Father has knit together the great family of man in one blessed bond of mutual need and mutual usefulness all over the world; so that no member of it can do without the other, and each member of it—each individual man—let him work at what thing he will, can make many times more of that thing than he needs for himself, and so help others while he earns his own living; and so wealth and comfort ought to increase year by year among the whole family of men, ay, and would increase, if it were not for sin. Yes, my friends, if it were not for that same sin—if it were not that men do not seek first the kingdom of God and His righteousness, there would be no end, no bound to the wealth, the comfort, the happiness of the children of men. Even as it is, in spite of all man's sin, the world does prosper marvellously, miraculously; in spite of all the waste, destruction, idleness, ignorance, injustice, and folly which goes on in the world, mankind increases and replenishes the earth, and improves in comfort and in happiness; in spite of all, God is stronger than the Devil, life stronger than death, wisdom stronger than folly, order stronger than disorder, fruitfulness stronger than destruction; and they will be so, more and more, till the last great day, when Christ shall have put all enemies under His feet, and death is swallowed up in victory, and all mankind is one fold under one Shepherd, Jesus Christ, the righteous King of all.

But some may ask, What does our Lord mean when He says, 'That if we sought first the kingdom of God and His righteousness, all these things should be added to us?'

I cannot tell you altogether, my friends; for eye hath not seen, nor ear heard, nor hath it entered into the heart of man to conceive what God has prepared for those who love Him. But this I can tell you, that these things are taken from men, instead of being added to them, by their not seeking first God's kingdom and His righteousness. I can tell you, as the Prophet does, that it is the sins of man which withhold good things from him; because though, as the Prophet says in the same place, God sends the good things, and the former and latter rain in their season, and reserves to men still the appointed weeks of harvest, yet men will not fear that same Lord their God; and therefore those good things are wasted, and mankind remains too often miserable in spite of God's goodness, and starving in the midst of God's plenty.

If you wish to know what I mean, look but once at this present war. I do not complain of the war. I honour the war. I thank God from the bottom of my heart for this great and glorious victory, and I call on you to thank Him, too, for it. I am none of those who think war sinful. I cannot do so, for I swore at my baptism to fight manfully under Christ's banner against the world, the flesh, and the Devil; and if we cannot reach the Devil and his works by any other means, we must reach them as we are doing now, by sharp shot and cold steel, and we must hold it an honourable thing, and few things more honourable on earth, for a man to die fighting against evil men, and an evil world-devouring empire, like that of Babylon of old, or this of Russia now, that he may save not merely us who sit here now, but our children's children, and generations yet unborn, from Russian tyranny, and Russian falsehood, and Russian profligacy, and Russian superstition. I say, I do not complain of this war; but I ask you to look at the mere waste which it brings, the mere waste of God's blessings. Consider all the skilful men now employed in making cannon, shot, and powder to kill mortal men, who might every one of them, in time of peace, have been employed in making things which would feed, and clothe, and comfort mortal man. Consider that very powder and shot itself, the fruit of so much labour and money, made simply to be shot away, once for all, as if a man should spend months in making some precious vessel, and then dash it to pieces the moment it was made. Consider that Sevastopol alone; the millions of money which it must have cost— the stone, the timber, the iron, all used there—in making a mere robber's den, which might all have been spent in giving employment and sustenance to whole provinces of poor starving Russians. Consider those tens of thousands of men, labouring day and night for months at those deadly earthworks, whose strong arms might have been all tilling God's earth, and growing food for the use of man. And then see the waste, the want, the misery which that one place, Sevastopol, has caused upon God's earth.

And consider, too, the souls of mortal men, who have been wasted there—no man knows how many, nor will know till the judgment day. Two hundred thousand, at the least, they say, wasted about that accursed place, within the last twelve months. Two hundred thousand cunning brains, two hundred thousand strong right hands, two hundred thousand willing hearts: what good might not each of those men have done if he had been labouring peacefully at home, in his right place in God's family! What might he not have invented, made, carried over land and sea? None dead there but might have been of use in his generation; and doubtless many a one who would have done good with all his might, who would have been a blessing to those around him; and now what is left of him on earth but a few bones beneath the sod? Wasted—utterly wasted! Oh, consider how precious is one man; consider how much good the weakest and stupidest of us all might do, if he set himself with his whole soul to do good; consider that the weakest and stupidest of us, even if he has no care for good, cannot earn his day's wages without doing some good to the bodies of his fellow-men; and then judge of the loss to mankind by this one single siege of one single town; and think how many stomachs must be the emptier, how many backs the barer, for this one war; and then see how man wastes God's gifts, and wastes most of all that most precious gift of all, men, living men, with minds, and reasons, and immortal souls.

And whence has all this waste come? Simply because these Russian rulers have chosen to seek first, not God's kingdom, but their own. Instead of behaving like God's ministers and God's stewards, and asking, 'How would God our King have us rule His kingdom?' they have laboured for their own power, conquering all the nations round them, removing their neighbour's landmark, and wasting the wealth of their country on armies, and fortresses, and fleets, with which they intended to conquer more and more of the earth which did not belong to them. Because, instead of seeking God's righteousness, and saying to themselves, 'How shall we be righteous, even as our Heavenly Father is righteous, and how shall we teach this great people to be righteous likewise?' they have sought their own pleasure, and lived in profligacy, covetous and cheating almost beyond belief; and instead of behaving righteously to the people, or teaching them to be righteous, they have crushed down the people, stupefied and corrupted them by slavery, and maddened them by superstitions which are not the righteousness of God, till they have made them easy tools in their unjust wars, and are able to drive them, even by force, like sheep to the slaughter, to die miserably in a cause in which, even if those unhappy slaves conquered, they would only rivet their own chains more tightly, and put more power into the hands of the very rulers who are robbing them of their earnings, dishonouring their daughters, and driving off their sons to die in a foreign land. Ah, my friends, if these men had but sought first the kingdom of God and His righteousness; if the great wealth, and the wonderful industry and prudence of Russia had been but spent in doing justly, and loving mercy, what a rich and honourable country of brave and industrious Christian men might Russia be; a blessing, and not a curse, to half the earth of God!

Let us pray that she will become so, some day; and we may have hope for her, for she is but young, and has time yet for repentance.

But some may say—indeed, we are all ready enough to say—'Then the evil of this war is the Russians' fault, and not ours; and so in every other case. In every other evil and misery they are rather other people's fault than ours. If we do our duty well enough, and if other people would but do theirs, all would be well.'

We are all apt to say this in our hearts. But our Lord does not say so. His promise is to all mankind: but His promise is to each of us also. When He says, Seek ye first God's kingdom and righteousness, He speaks to you and to me, to every soul now here. Believe it, my friends. The more that I see of life, the more I see how much of our sorrow is our own fault; how much of our happiness is in our own hands; and the more I see how little use there is in finding fault with this government, or that, the more I see how much use there is in every man's finding fault with himself, and taking his share of the blame.

I do not doubt that if the whole people of England, for the last forty years, had sought first God's kingdom and God's righteousness, and said to themselves in every matter, not merely 'What is profitable for us to do?' but 'What is right for us to do?' we should have been spared the expenses and the sorrows of this war: but as for blaming our government, my friends,—what they are we are; we choose them, Englishmen like ourselves, and they truly represent us. Not one complaint can we make against them, which we may not as justly make against ourselves; and if we had been in their places, we should have done what they did; for the seeds of the same sins are in us; and we yield, each in his own household and his own business, to the same temptations as they, to the sins which so easily beset Englishmen at this present time. I say, frankly, I see not one charge brought against them in the newspapers which might not quite as justly be brought against me, and, for aught I know, against every one of us here; and while we are not faithful over a few things, what right have we to complain of them for not having been faithful over many things? Believe, rather (I believe it), that if we had been in their place, we should have done far worse than they; and ask yourselves, 'Do I seek first God's kingdom and God's righteousness; for if I do not, what right have I to lay the blame of my bad success on other men's not seeking them?' To each of us, as much as to our government, or to the Russian empire, is Christ's command; and each of us must take the consequences, if we break it. Let us look at ourselves, and mend ourselves, and try whether God's promise will not hold true for us, each in his station, let the world round us go as it will. Be sure that God is just, and that every man bears his own burden: that the righteous should be as the wicked, that be far from Thee, O God! Shall not the judge of all the earth do right? Be sure that those who trust in Him shall never be confounded, though the earth be moved, and the mountains carried into the midst of the sea, as it is written, 'Trust in the Lord, and be doing good; dwell in the land, and work where God has placed thee, and verily thou shalt be fed.'

But have we done so, my friends? have we sought first God's kingdom and His righteousness? have we not rather forgotten the meaning of the text, and what God's kingdom is, and what His righteousness is? Do not most people fancy that God's kingdom only means some pleasant place to which people are to go after they die? and that seeking God's righteousness only means having Christ's righteousness imputed to us (as they call it), without our being righteous and good ourselves? Do not most of us fancy that this very text means, 'Do you take care of your souls, and God will take care of your bodies; do you see after the salvation of your souls, and God will see after the salvation of your bodies'? a meaning which, in the first place, is not true, for God will do no such thing; and all the religion in the world will not prevent a man's having to work for his daily bread, or pay his debts for him without money; and a meaning which, in the second place, people themselves do not believe; for religious professors in general now are just as keen about money as irreligious ones, and even more so; so that covetousness and cunning, ambition and greediness to rise in life, seem now-a-days to go hand in hand with a high religious profession; and those who fancy themselves the children of light have become just as wise in their generation as the children of this world whom they despise.

No, my friends, that is not the meaning of the text; and when I ask you, Have you obeyed the text? I do not ask you that question; but one which I believe is something far more spiritual and more deep, something at least which is far more heart-searching, and likely to prick a man's conscience, perhaps to make him angry with me who ask.

Do you seek first God's kingdom, or your own profit, your own pleasure, your own reputation? Do you believe that you are in God's kingdom, that He is your King, and has called you to the station in which you are to do good and useful work for Him upon this earth of His? Whatever be your calling, whether you be servant, labourer, farmer, tradesman, gentleman, maid, wife, or widow, father, son, or husband, do you ask yourself every day, 'Now what are the laws of God's kingdom about this station of mine? what is my duty here? how can I obey God, and His laws here, and do what He requires of me, and so be a good servant, a good labourer, a good tradesman, a good master, a good parish officer, a good wife, a good parent, pleasing to God, useful to my neighbours and to my countrymen?' Or do you say to yourselves, 'How can I get the greatest quantity of money and pleasure out of my station, with the least trouble to myself?' My dearest friends, ask yourselves, each of you, in which of these two ways do you look at your own station in life?

And do you seek first God's righteousness? There can be no mistake as to what God's righteousness is; for God's righteousness must be Christ's righteousness, seeing that He is the express image of His Father. Now do you ask yourselves, 'How am I to be righteous in my station, as Christ was in His? how can I do my Heavenly Father's will, as Christ did? how can I behave like Christ in my station? how would the Lord Jesus Christ have behaved, if He had been in my place, when He was on earth?' My friends, that is the question, the searching question, the question which must convince us all of sin, and show us so many faults of our own to complain of, that we shall find no time to throw stones at our neighbours. How would the Lord Jesus Christ have behaved, if He had been in my place when He was upon earth?

My dear friends, till we can all of us answer that question somewhat better than we can now, we have no need to look as far as Russia, or as our forefathers' mistakes, or our rulers' mistakes, to find out why this trouble and that trouble come upon us: for we shall find the reason in our own selfish, greedy, self-willed hearts.

Oh, my friends, let us each search our own lives, and repent, and amend, and resolve to do our duty, as sons of God, in the station to which God has called us, by the help of the Spirit of God, which He has promised freely to those who ask Him. And now, this day, as we thank God for this great victory, let us thank Him, not with our lips merely, but with our lives, by living such lives as He loves to see, such lives as He meant us to live, lives of loyalty to God, and of usefulness to our brethren, and of industry and prudence in our calling, and so help forward, each of us, however humble our station, the glory of God; because we shall each of us, in the cottage and in the field, in the shop and in the mansion, in this our little parish, and therefore in the great nation of which it is a part, help forward the fulfilment of those blessed words, Our Father which art in heaven; Thy kingdom come; Thy will be done on earth as it is in heaven; and therefore, also, the fulfilment of the words which come after them, and not before them; Give us this day our daily bread.

SERMON XIV

ENGLAND'S STRENGTH

I will defend this city, to save it for mine own sake.

2 Kings xix. 34.

The first lesson for this morning's service is of the grandest in the whole Old Testament; grander perhaps than all, except the story of the passage of the Red Sea, and the giving of the Law on Sinai. It follows out the story which you heard in the first lesson for last Sunday afternoon, of the invasion of Judea by the Assyrians. You heard then how this great Assyrian conqueror, Sennacherib, after taking all the fortified towns of Judah, and sweeping the whole country with fire and sword, sent three of his generals up to the very walls of Jerusalem, commanding King Hezekiah to surrender at discretion, and throw himself and his people on Sennacherib's mercy; how proudly and boastfully he taunted the Jews with their weakness; how, like the Russian emperor now, he called in religion as the excuse for his conquests and robberies, saying, as if God's blessings were on them, 'Am I now come up without the Lord against this place to destroy it? The Lord said to me, Go up against this place to destroy it;' while all the time what he really trusted in (as his own words showed) was what the Russian emperors trust in, their own strength and the number of their armies.

Jerusalem was thus in utter need and danger; the vast army of the Assyrians was encamped at Lachish, not more than ten miles off; and however strong the walls of Jerusalem might be, and however advantageously it might stand on its high hill, with lofty rocks and cliffs on three sides of it, yet Hezekiah knew well that no strength of his could stand more than a few days against Sennacherib's army. For these Assyrians had brought the art of war to a greater perfection than any nation of the old world: they lived for war, and studied, it seems, only how to conquer. And they have left behind them very remarkable proofs of what sort of men they were, of which I think it right to tell you all; for they are most instructive, not merely because they prove the truth of Isaiah's account, but because they explain it, and help us in many ways to understand his prophecies. They are a number of sculptures and paintings, representing Sennacherib, his army, and his different conquests, which were painted by his command, in his palace; and having been lately discovered there, among the ruins of Nineveh, have been brought to England, and are now in the British Museum, while copies of many of them are in the Crystal Palace. There we see these terrible Assyrian conquerors defeating their enemies, torturing and slaughtering their prisoners, swimming rivers, beating down castles, sweeping on from land to land like a devouring fire, while over their heads fly fierce spirits who protect and prosper their cruelties, and eagles who trail in their claws the entrails of the slain. The very expression of their faces is frightful for its fierceness; the countenances of a 'bitter and hasty nation,' as the Prophet calls them, whose feet were swift to shed blood. And as for the art of war, and their power of taking walled towns like Jerusalem, you may see them in these pictures battering down and undermining forts and castles, with instruments so well made and powerful, that all other nations who came after them, for more than two thousand years, seem to have been content to copy from them, and hardly to have improved on the old Assyrian engines.

Such, and so terrible, they came up against Jerusalem: to attempt to fight them would have been useless madness; and Hezekiah had but one means of escaping from them, and that was to cast himself and his people upon the boundless mercy, and faithfulness, and power of God.

And Hezekiah had his answer by Isaiah the prophet: and more than an answer. The Lord took the matter into His own hand, and showed Sennacherib which was the stronger, his soldiers and horses and engines, or the Lord God; and so that terrible Assyrian army came utterly to nought, and vanished off the face of the earth.

Now, my friends, has this noble history no lesson in it for us? God forbid! It has a lesson which ought to come nearer to our hearts than to the hearts of any nation: for though we or our forefathers have never been, for nearly three hundred years, in such utter need and danger as Jerusalem was, yet be sure that we might have been so, again and again, had it not been for the mercy of the same God who delivered Jerusalem from the Assyrians. It is now three hundred years ago that the Lord delivered this country from as terrible an invader as Sennacherib himself; when He three times scattered by storms the fleets of the King of Spain, which were coming to lay waste this land with fire and sword: and since then no foreign foe has set foot on English soil, and we almost alone, of all the nations of Europe, have been preserved from those horrors of war, even to speak of which is dreadful! Oh, my friends! we know not half God's goodness to us!

And if you ask me, why God has so blest and favoured this land, I can only answer—and I am not ashamed or afraid to answer—I believe it is on account of the Church of England; it is because God has put His name here in a peculiar way, as He did among the Jews of old, and that He is jealous for His Church, and for the special knowledge of His Gospel and His Law, which He has given us in our Prayer-book and in our Church Catechism, lighting therein a candle in England which I believe will never be put out. It is not merely that we are a Protestant country,—great blessing as that is,—it is, I believe, that there is something in the Church of England which there is not in Protestant countries abroad, unless perhaps Sweden: for every one of them (except Sweden and ourselves) has suffered, from time to time, invading armies, and the unspeakable horrors of war. In some of them the light of the Gospel has been quenched utterly, and in others it lingers like a candle flickering down into the socket. By horrible persecutions, and murder, and war, and pillage, have those nations been tormented from time to time; and who are we, that we should escape? Certainly from no righteousness of our own. Some may say, It is our great wealth which has made us strong. My friends, believe it not. Look at Spain, which was once the richest of all nations; and did her riches preserve her? Has she not dwindled down into the most miserable and helpless of all nations? Has not her very wealth vanished from her, because she sold herself to work all unrighteousness with greediness?

Some may say, It is our freedom which makes us strong. My friends, believe it not. Freedom is a vast blessing from God, but freedom alone will preserve no nation. How many free nations have fallen into every sort of misery, ay, into bitter slavery, in spite of all their freedom. How many free nations in Europe lie now in bondage, gnawing their tongues for pain, and weary with waiting for the deliverance which does not come? No, my friends, freedom is of little use without something else—and that is loyalty; reverence for law and obedience to the powers that be, because men believe those powers to be ordained of God; because men believe that Christ is their King, and they His ministers and stewards, and that He it is who appoints all orders and degrees of men in His Holy Church. True freedom can only live with true loyalty and obedience, such as our Prayer-book, our Catechism, our Church of England preaches to us. It is a Church meant for free men, who stand each face to face with their Heavenly Father: but it is a Church meant also for loyal men, who look on the law as the ordinance of God, and on their rulers as the ministers of God; and if our freedom has had anything to do (as no doubt it has) with our prosperity, I believe that we owe the greater part of our freedom to the teaching and the general tone of mind which our Prayer-book has given to us and to our forefathers for now three hundred years.

Not that we have listened to that teaching, or acted up to it: God knows, we have been but too like the Jews in Isaiah's time, who had the Law of God, and yet did every man what was right in his own eyes; we, like them, have been hypocritical; we, like them, have neglected the poor, and the widow, and the orphan; we, like them, have been too apt to pay tithe of mint and anise, and neglect the weightier matters of the law, justice, mercy, and judgment. When we read that awful first chapter of Isaiah, we may well tremble; for all the charges which he brings against the Jews of his time would just as well apply to us; but yet we can trust in the Lord, as Isaiah did, and believe that He will be jealous for His land, and for His name's sake, and not suffer the nations to say of us, 'Where is now their God?' We can trust Him, that if He turn His hand on us, as He did on the Jews of old, and bring us into danger and trouble, yet it will be in love and mercy, that He may purge away our dross, and take away all our alloy, and restore our rulers as at the first, and our counsellors as at the beginning, that we may be called, 'The city of righteousness, the faithful city.' True, we must not fancy that we have any righteousness of our own, that we merit God's favour above other people; our consciences ought to tell us that cannot be; our Bibles tell us that is an empty boast. Did we not hear this morning, 'Bring forth fruits meet for repentance: and think not to say within yourselves, We have Abraham to our father; for God is able of these stones to raise up children to Abraham.' But we may comfort ourselves with the thought that there is One standing among us (though we see Him not) who will, ay, and does, 'baptize us with the Holy Ghost and with fire, whose fan is in His hand, and He will thoroughly purge His floor, and gather the wheat into His garner,' for the use of our children after us, and the generations yet unborn, while the chaff, all among us which is empty, and light, and rotten, and useless, He will burn up (thanks be to His holy name) with fire unquenchable, which neither the falsehood and folly of man, nor the malice of the Devil, can put out, but which will purge this land of all its sins.

This is our hope, and this is the cause of our thankfulness. For who but we should be thankful this day that we are Englishmen, members of Christ's Church of England, inhabitants of, perhaps, the only country in Europe which is not now perplexed with fear of change, while men's hearts fail them for dread, and looking for those things which are coming on the earth? a country which has never seen, as all the countries round have seen, a foreign army trampling down their crops, burning their farms, cutting down their trees, plundering their towns, destroying in a day the labour of years, while women are dishonoured, men tortured to make them give up their money, the able-bodied driven from their homes, ruined and wanderers, and the sick and aged left to perish of famine and neglect. My friends, all these things were going on but last year upon the Danube. They are going on now in Asia: even with all the mercy and moderation of our soldiers and sailors, we have not been able to avoid inflicting some of these very miseries upon our own enemies; and yet here we are, going about our business in peace and safety in a land in which we and our forefathers have found, now for many a year, that just laws make a quiet and prosperous people; that the effect of righteousness is peace, and the fruit of righteousness, quietness and assurance for ever;—a land in which the good are not terrified, the industrious hampered, and the greedy and lawless made eager and restless by expectation of change in government; but every man can boldly and hopefully work in his calling, and 'whatsoever his hand finds to do, do it with all his might,' in fair hope that the money which he earns in his manhood he will be able to enjoy quietly in his old age, and hand it down safely to his children, and his children's children;—a land which for hundreds of years has not felt the unspeakable horrors of war; a land which even now is safely and peacefully gathering in its harvest, while so many countries lie wasted with fire and sword. Oh, my friends, who made us to differ from others, or what have we that we did not receive? Not to ourselves do we owe our blessings; hardly even to our wise forefathers: but to God Himself, and the Spirit of God which was with them, and is with us still, in spite of all our shortcomings. We owe it to our wise Constitution, to our wise Church, the principle of which is that God is Judge and Christ is King, in peace as well as in war, in times of quiet as well as in times of change; I say, to our wise Constitution and to our wise Church, which teach us that all power is of God; that all men who have power, great or small, are His stewards; that all orders and degrees of men in His Holy Church, from the queen on the throne to the labourer in the harvest-field, are called by God to their ministry and vocation, and are responsible to God for their conduct therein. How then shall we show forth our thankfulness, not only in our lips, but in our lives? How, but by believing that very principle, that very truth which He has taught us, and by which England stands, that we are God's people, and God's servants? He has indeed showed us what is good, and our fathers before us; and what does the Lord require of us in return, but to do the good which He has showed us, to do justly, to love mercy, and to walk humbly with our God?

Oh, my friends, come frankly and joyfully to the Lord's Table

this day. Confess your sins and shortcomings to Him, and entreat
Him to enable you to live more worthily of your many blessings.
Offer to Him the sacrifice of your praise and thankfulness, imperfect
though it is, and join with angels and archangels in blessing Him for
what He is, and what He has been to you: and then receive your
share of His most perfect sacrifice of praise and thanksgiving, the
bread and the wine which tell you that you are members of His
Church; that His body gives you whatsoever life and strength your
souls have; that His blood washes out all your sins and
shortcomings; that His Spirit shall be renewed in you day by day, to
teach you to do the good work which He has prepared already for
you, and to walk in the old paths which have led our forefathers,
and will lead us too, I trust, safe through the chances and changes of
this mortal life, and the fall of mighty kingdoms, towards that
perfect City of God which is eternal in the heavens.

SERMON XV

THE LIFE OF GOD

That ye walk not as other Gentiles walk, in the vanity of their mind, being alienated from the life of God through the ignorance that is in them, because of the blindness of their heart.

Ephesians iv. 17, 18.

You heard these words read in the Epistle for to-day. I cannot expect that you all understood them. It is no shame to you that you did not. Some of them are long and hard Latin words. Some of them, though they are plain English enough, are hard to understand because they have to do with deep matters, which can only be understood by the help of God's Spirit. And even with the help of God's Spirit we cannot any of us expect to understand all which they mean: we cannot expect to be as wise as St. Paul; for we must be as good as St. Paul before we can be as wise about goodness as he was. I do not pretend to understand all the text myself: no, not half, nor a tenth part of what it very likely means. But I do seem to myself to understand a little about it, by the help and blessing of God; and what little of it I do understand, I will try to make you understand also.

For the words in the text belong to you as much as to me, or to St. Paul himself. What is true for one man, is true for every man. What is right for one man, is right for every man. What God promises for one man, He promises to every man. Man or woman, black or white, rich or poor, scholar or unlearned, there is no respect of persons with Him. 'In Christ Jesus,' says St. Paul, 'there is neither male nor female, slave nor freeman, Jew who fancies that God's promises belong to him alone, or Gentile who knows nothing about them, clever learned Greek, or stupid ignorant Barbarian.'

It is enough for God that we are all men and women bearing the flesh, and blood, and human nature which His Son Jesus Christ wore on earth. If we are baptized, we belong to Him: if we are not baptized, we ought to be; for we belong to Him just as much. Every man may be baptized; every man may be regenerate; God calls all to His grace and adoption and holy baptism, which is the sign and seal of His adoption; and therefore, what is right for the regenerate

114

baptized man, is right for the unregenerate unbaptized man; for the Christian and for the heathen there is but one way, one duty, one life for both, and that is the life of God, of which St. Paul speaks in the text.

Now of this life of God I will speak hereafter; but I mention it now, because it is the thing to which I wish to bring your thoughts before the end of the sermon.

But first, let us see what St. Paul means, when he talks about the Gentiles in his day. For that also has to do with us. I said that every man, Christian or heathen, has the same duty, and is bound to do the same right; every man, Christian or heathen, if he sins, breaks his duty in the same way, and does the same wrong. There is but one righteousness, the life of God; there is but one sin, and that is being alienated from the life of God. One man may commit different sorts of sins from another; one may lie, another may steal: one may be proud, another may be covetous: but all these different sins come from the same root of sin; they are all flowers of the same plant. And St. Paul tells us what that one root of sin, what that same Devil's plant, is, which produces all sin in Christian or Heathen, in Churchman or Dissenter, in man or woman—the one disease, from which has come all the sin which ever was done by man, woman, or child since the world was made.

Now, what is this one disease, to which every man, you and I, are all liable? Why it is that we are every one of us worse than we ought to be, worse than we know how to be, and, strangest of all, worse than we wish and like to be.

Just as far as we are like the heathen of old, we shall be worse than we know how to be. For we are all ready enough to turn heathens again, at any moment, my friends; and the best Christian in this church knows best that what I say is true; that he is beset by the very same temptations which ruined the old heathens, and that if he gave way to them a moment they would ruin him likewise. For what does St. Paul say was the matter with the old heathens?

First he says, 'Their understanding was darkened.' But what part of it? What was it that they had got dark about and could not understand? For in some matters they were as clever as we, and cleverer. What part of their understanding was it which was darkened? St. Paul tells us in the first chapter of the Epistle to the Romans. It was their hearts—their reason, as we should say. It was about God, and the life of God, that they were dark. They had not been always dark about God, but they were darkened; they grew more and more dark about Him, generation after generation; they gave themselves up more and more to their corrupt and fallen nature, and so the children grew worse than their fathers, and their children again worse than them, till they had lost all notion of what God was like. For from the very first all heathens have had some notion of what God is like, and have had a notion also, which none but God could have given them, that men ought to be like God. God taught, or if I may so speak, tried to teach, the heathen, from the very first. If God had not taught them, they would not have been to blame for knowing nothing of God. For as Job says, 'Can man by searching find out God?' Surely not; God must teach us about Himself. Never forget that man cannot find God; God must show Himself to man of His own free grace and will. God must reveal and unveil Himself to us, or we shall never even fancy that there is a God. And God did so to the heathen. Even before the Flood, God's Spirit strove with man; and after the Flood we read how the Lord, Jesus Christ the Son of God, revealed Himself in many different ways to heathens. To Pharaoh, king of Egypt, in Abraham's times; and again to Abimelech, king of Gerar; and again to Pharaoh and his servants, in Joseph's time; and to Nebuchadnezzar, king of Babylon, and to Cyrus, king of Persia; and no doubt to thousands more. Indeed, no man, heathen or Christian, ever thought a single true thought, or felt a single right feeling, about God or man, or man's duty to God and his neighbour, unless God revealed it to him (whether or not He also revealed Himself to the man and showed him who it was who was putting the right thought into his mind): for every right thought and feeling about God, and goodness, and duty, are the very voice of God Himself, the word of God whereof St. John speaks, and Moses and the prophets speak, speaking to the heart of sinful man, to enlighten and to teach him. And therefore, St. Paul says, the sinful heathen were without excuse, because, he says, 'that which may be known of God is manifest, that is plain, among them, for God hath showed it to them. For the invisible things of Him from the creation of the world are clearly seen, being understood by the things which are made, even His eternal power and Godhead; so that they are without excuse.' 'But these heathens,' he says, 'did not like to retain God in their knowledge; and when they knew God, did not glorify Him as God, and changed the glory of the Incorruptible God into the likeness of corruptible man, and beasts and creeping things.' And so they were alienated from the life of God; that is, they became strangers to God's life; they forgot what God's life and character was like: or if they even did awake a moment, and recollect dimly what God was like, they hated that thought. They hated to think that God was what He was, and shut their eyes, and stopped their ears as fast as possible.

And what happened to them in the meantime? What was the fruit of their wilfully forgetting what God's life was? St. Paul tells us that they fell into the most horrible sins—sins too dreadful and shameful to be spoken of; and that their common life, even when they did not run into such fearful evils, was profligate, fierce, and miserable. And yet St. Paul tells us all the while they knew the judgment of God, that those who do such things are worthy of death.

Now we know that St. Paul speaks truth, from the writings of heathens; for God raised up from time to time, even among the heathen Greeks and Romans, witnesses for Himself, to testify of Him and of His life, and to testify against the sins of the world, such men as Socrates and Plato among the Greeks, whose writings St. Paul knew thoroughly, and whom, I have no doubt, he had in his mind when he wrote his first chapter of Romans, and told the heathen that they were without excuse. And among the Romans, also, He raised up, in the same way, witnesses for Himself, such as Juvenal and Persius, and others, whom scholars know well. And to these men, heathens though they were, God certainly did teach a great deal about Himself, and gave them courage to rebuke the sins of kings and rich men, even at the danger of their lives; and to some of them he gave courage even to suffer martyrdom for the message which God had given them, and which their neighbours hated to hear. And this was the message which God sent by them to the heathen: that God was good and righteous, and that therefore His everlasting wrath must be awaiting sinners. They rebuked their heathen neighbours for those very same horrible crimes which St. Paul mentions; and then they said, as St. Paul does, 'How you make your own sins worse by blasphemies against God! You sin yourselves, and then, to excuse yourselves, you invent fables and lies about God, and pretend that God is as wicked as you are, in order to drug your own consciences, by making God the pattern of your own wickedness.'

These men saw that man ought to be like God; and they saw that God was righteous and good; and they saw, therefore, that unrighteousness and sin must end in ruin and everlasting misery. So much God had taught them, but not much more; but to St. Paul he had taught more. Those wise and righteous heathen could show their sinful neighbours that sin was death, and that God was righteous. But they could not tell them how to rise out of the death of sin, into God's life of righteousness. They could preach the terrors of the Law, but they did not know the good news of the Gospel, and therefore they did not succeed; they did not convert their neighbours to God. Then came St. Paul and preached to the very same people, and he did convert them to God; for he had good news for them, of things which prophets and kings had desired to see, and had not seen them, and to hear, and had not heard them.

For God, who at sundry times and in divers manners spoke to the fathers by the prophets, at last spoke to all men by a Son, His only-begotten Son, the exact likeness of His Father, the brightness of His glory, and the express image of His person. He sent Him to be a man: very man of the substance of His mother, the Blessed Virgin Mary, at the same time that He was Very God, of the substance of His Father, begotten before all worlds.

And so God, and the life of God, was manifested in the flesh and reasonable soul of a man; and from that time there is no doubt what the life of God is; for the life of God is the life of Jesus Christ. There is no doubt now what God is like, for God is like Jesus Christ. No one can now say, 'I cannot see God, how then can you expect me to be like God?' for He who has seen Jesus Christ, as His character stands in the Gospels, has seen God the Father. No one can say now, 'How can a man be like God, and live a life like God's life?' for if any one of you say that, I can answer him: 'A man can be like God; you can be like God; for there was once a man on earth, Jesus, the son of the Blessed Virgin, who was perfectly like God.' And if you answer, 'But He was like God, because He was God,' I can say, 'And that is the very reason why you can be like God also.' If Jesus Christ had been only a man, you could no more become like Him than you can become clever because another man is clever, or strong because another man is strong: but because He was God The Son of God, He can give you, to make you like God, the same Holy Spirit which made Him like God; for that Holy Spirit proceeds from Him, the Son, as well as from the Father, and the Father has committed all power to the Son; and therefore that same Man Christ Jesus has power to change your heart, and renew it, and shape it to be like Him, and like His Father, by the power of His Spirit, that you may be like God as He was like God, and live the life of God which He lived; so that the Lord Jesus Christ, because He was a man like God, showed that all men can become like God; and because He was God, Very God of Very God, He is able to make all who come to Him men like Himself, men like God, and raise them up body and soul to the everlasting life of God, that He may be the firstborn among many brethren.

Now what is this everlasting life of God, which the Lord Jesus Christ lived perfectly, and which He can and will make every one of us live, in proportion as we give up our hearts and wills to Him, and ask Him to take charge of us, and shape us, and teach us? When we read that blessed story of Him who was born in a stable, and laid in a manger, who went about doing good, because God was with Him, who condescended of His own freewill to be mocked, and scourged, and spit upon, and crucified, that He might take away the sins of the whole world, who prayed for His murderers, and blest those who cursed Him—what sort of life does this life of God, which He lived, seem to us? Is it not a life of love, joy, peace, long-suffering, gentleness, goodness, patience, meekness? Surely it is; then that is the likeness of God. God is love. And the Lord Jesus' life was a life of love—utter, perfect, untiring love. He did His Father's will perfectly, because He loved men perfectly, and to the death. He died for those who hated Him, and so He showed forth to man the name and glory of God; for God is love. The name of the Father, and of the Son, and of the Holy Ghost is love; for love is justice and righteousness, as it is written, 'Love worketh no ill to his neighbour: therefore love is the fulfilling of the law.' And God is perfect love, because He is perfect righteousness; and perfect righteousness, because He is perfect love; for His love and His justice are not two different things, two different parts of God, as some say, who fancy that God's justice had to be satisfied in one way, and His love in another, and talk of God as if His justice fought against His love, and desired the death of a sinner, and then His love fought against His justice, and desired to save a sinner. No wonder that those who hold such doctrines go further still, and talk as if God the Father desired to destroy mankind, and would have done it if God the Son had not interposed, and suffered Himself instead; till they can fancy that they are Christians, and know God, while they use the hideous words of a certain hymn, which speaks of

> 'The streaming drops of Jesu's blood
> Which calmed the Father's frowning face.'

May God deliver and preserve us and our children from all such blasphemous fables, which, like the fables of the old heathen, change the glory of the Incorruptible God into the likeness of a corruptible man, which deny the true faith, that God has neither parts nor passions, by talking of His love and His justice as two different things; which confound His persons by saying that the Son alone does what the Father and the Holy Spirit do also, while they divide His substance by making the will of the Son different from the will of the Father, and deny that such as the Father is, such is the Son, and such is the Holy Ghost, all three one perfect Love, and one perfect Justice, because they are all three one God, and God is love, and love is righteousness.

Believe me, my friends, this is no mere question of words, which only has to do with scholars in their libraries; it is a question, the question of life and death for you, and me, and every living soul in this church,—Do we know what the life of God is? are we living it? or are we alienated from it, careless about it, disliking it?

For, as I said at the beginning of my sermon, we are all ready enough to turn heathens again; and if we grow to forget or dislike the life of God, we shall be heathen at heart. We may talk about Him with our lips, we may quarrel and curse each other about religious differences; but let us make as great a profession as we may, if we do not love the life of God we shall be heathen at heart, and we shall, sooner or later, fall into sin. The heathens fell into sin just in proportion as their hearts were turned away from the life of God, and so shall we. And how shall we know whether our hearts are turned away, or whether they are right with God? Thus: What are the fruits of God's Spirit? what sort of life does the Spirit of God make man live? For the Spirit of God is God, and therefore the life of God is the life which God's Spirit makes men live; and what is that? a life of love and righteousness.

The old heathens did not like such a life, therefore they did not like to retain God in their knowledge. They knew that man ought to be like God: and St. Paul says, they ought to have known what God was like; that He was Love; for St. Paul told them He left not Himself without witness, in that He sent them rain and fruitful seasons, filling their hearts with food and gladness. That was, in St. Paul's eyes, God's plainest witness of Himself—the sign that God was Love, making His sun shine on the just and on the unjust, and good to the unthankful and the evil—in one word, perfect, because He is perfect Love. But they preferred to be selfish, covetous, envious, revengeful, delighting to indulge themselves in filthy pleasures, to oppress and defraud each other. Do you?

For you can, I can, every baptized man can take his choice between the selfish life of the heathens and the loving life of God: we may either keep to the old pattern of man, which is corrupt according to the deceitful lusts; or we may put on the new pattern of man, which is after God's likeness, and founded upon righteousness and truthful holiness.

Every baptized man may choose. For he is not only bound to live the life of God: every man, as the old heathen philosophers knew, is bound to live it: but more. The baptized man can live it: that is the good news of his baptism. You can live the life of God, for you know what the life of God is—it is the life of Jesus Christ. You can live the life of God, for the Spirit of God is with you, to cleanse your soul and life, day by day, till they are like the soul and life of Christ.

Then you will be, as the apostle says, 'a partaker of a divine nature.' Then—and it is an awful thing to say—a thing past hope, past belief, but I must say it—for it is in the Bible, it is the word of the Blessed Lord Himself, and of His beloved apostle, St. John: 'If a man love Me, he will keep my commandments, and my Father will love him, and we will come to him and make our abode with him.' 'And this is His commandment,' says St. John, 'That we should love one another.' 'God is Love, and he who dwelleth in Love dwelleth in God, and God in him.'

God is Love. As I told you just now, the heathens of old might have known that, if they had chosen to open their eyes and see. But they would not see. They were dark, cruel, and unloving, and therefore they fancied that God was dark, cruel, and unloving also. They did not love Love, and therefore they did not love God, for God is Love. And therefore they did not love loving: they did not enjoy loving; and so they lost the Spirit of God, which is the Spirit of Love. And therefore they did not love each other, but lived in hatred and suspicion, and selfishness, and darkness. They were but heathen. But if even they ought to have known that God was Love, how much more we? For we know of a deed of God's love, such as those poor heathen never dreamed of. God so loved the world, that He gave His only-begotten Son to die for it. Then God showed what His eternal life was—a life of love: then God showed what our eternal life is—to know Him who is Love, and Jesus Christ, whom He sent to show forth His love: then God showed that it is the duty and in the power of every man to live the life of God, the life of Love; for He sent forth into the world His Spirit, the Spirit of Love, to fill with love the heart of every man and woman who sees that Love is the image of God, and longs to be loving, and therefore longs to be like God; as it is written, 'Blessed are those who hunger and thirst after righteousness, for they shall be filled:' for righteousness is keeping Christ's commandment, and Christ's commandment is, that we love one another. And to those who long to do that, God's Spirit will come to fill them with love; and where the Spirit of God is, there is also the Father, and there is also the Son; for God's substance cannot be divided, as the Athanasian creed tells us (and blessed and cheering words they are); and he who hath the Holy Spirit of Love with him hath both the Father and the Son; as it is written: 'If a man love Me, my Father will love him, and we will come unto him, and make our abode with him.'

And then, if we have God abiding with us, and filling us with His Eternal Life, what more do we need for life, or death, or eternity, or eternities of eternities? For we shall live in and with and by God, who can never die or change, an everlasting life of love, whereof St. Paul says, that though prophecies shall fail, and tongues shall cease, and knowledge shall vanish away, because all that we know now is but in part, and all that we see now is through a glass darkly, yet Love shall never fail, but abide for ever and ever.

SERMON XVI

GOD'S OFFSPRING

*Wherefore thou art no more a servant, but a son; and
if a son, then an heir of God through Christ.*

Galatians iv. 7.

I say, writes St. Paul, in the epistle which you heard read just
now, 'that the heir, as long as he is a child, differs nothing from a
servant, though he be lord of all; but is under tutors and governors,
until the time appointed by his father. Even so,' he says, we, 'when
we were children, were in bondage under the elements of the world:
but when the fulness of time was come, God sent forth His Son
made of a woman, made under a law, to redeem them that were
under a law, that we might receive the adoption of sons.'

When we were children. He is not speaking of the Jews only;
for these Galatians to whom he was writing were not Jews at all, any
more than we are. He was speaking to men simply as men. He was
speaking to the Galatians as we have a right to speak to all men.

Nor does he mean merely when we were children in age. The
Greek word which he uses, means infants, people not come to years
of discretion. Indeed, the word which he uses means very often a
simpleton, an ignorant or foolish person; one who does not know
who and what he is, what is his duty, or how to do it.

Now this, he says, was the state of men before Christ came; this
is the state of all men by nature still; the state of all poor heathens,
whether in England or in foreign countries.

They are children—that is, ignorant and unable to take care of
themselves; because they do not know what they are. St. Paul tells
us what they are. That they are all God's offspring, though they
know it not. He likens them to young children, who, though they
are their father's heirs, have no more liberty than slaves have; but
are kept under tutors and masters, till they have arrived at years of
discretion, and are fit to take their places as their father's sons, and
to go out into the world, and have the management of their own
affairs, and a share in their father's property, which they may use
for themselves, instead of being merely fed and clothed by, and kept
in subjection to him, whether they will or not. This is what he

means by receiving the adoption of sons. He does not mean that we are not God's children till we find out that we are God's children. That is what some people say; but that is the very exact contrary to what St. Paul used to say. He told the heathen Athenians that they were God's children. He put them in mind that one of their own heathen poets had told them so, and had said, 'We are also God's offspring.' And so in this chapter he says, You were God's children all along, though you did not know it. You were God's heirs all along, although you differed nothing from slaves; for as long as you were in your heathen ignorance and foolishness, God had to treat you as His slaves, not as His children; and so you were in bondage under the elements of the world, till the fulness of time was come.

And, then, God sent His Son, born of a woman, born under a law, to redeem those who were under a law—that is, all mankind. The Jews were keeping, or pretending to keep, Moses' law, and trying to please God by that. The heathens were keeping all manner of old superstitious laws and customs about religion which their forefathers had handed down to them. But heathens, and indeed Jews too, at that time, all agreed in one thing. These laws and customs of theirs about religion all went upon the notion of their being God's slaves, and not his children. They thought that God did not love them; that they must buy His favours. They thought religion meant a plan for making God love them.

Then appeared the love of God in Jesus Christ. As at this very Christmas time, the Son of God, Jesus Christ the Lord, in whose likeness man was made at the beginning, was born into the world, to redeem us and all mankind. He told them of their Heavenly Father; He preached to them the good news of the kingdom of God; that God had not forgotten them, did not hate them, would freely forgive them all that was past; and why? Because He was their Father, and loved them, and loved them so that He spared not His only begotten Son, but freely gave Him for them. And now God looks at us human beings, not as we are in ourselves, sinful and corrupt, but he looks at us in the light of Jesus Christ, who has taken our nature upon Him, and redeemed it, and raised it up again, so that God can look on it now without disgust, and henceforth no one need be ashamed of being a man; for to be a man is to be in the likeness of God. Man was created in the image and likeness of God, and who is the image and likeness of God but Jesus Christ? Therefore man was created at first in Jesus Christ, and now, as St. Paul says, he is created anew in Jesus Christ; and now to be a man is to partake of the same flesh and blood which the Lord Jesus Christ wore for us, when He was made very man of the substance of his mother, and that without spot of sin, to show that man need not be sinful, that man was meant by God to be holy and pure from sin, and that by the Holy Spirit of Jesus Christ we, every one of us, can become pure from sin. This is the blessedness of Christmas-day. That one man, at least, has been born into the world spotless and free from sin, that He might be the firstborn of many brethren. This is the good news of Christmas-day. That now, in Christ's light, and for Christ's sake, our Father looks on us as His sons, and not His slaves.

Therefore is every child who comes into the world baptized freely into the name of God. Baptism is a sign and warrant that God loves that child; that God looks on it as His child, not for itself or its own sake, but because it belongs to Jesus Christ, who, by becoming a man, redeemed all mankind, and made them His property and His brothers. Therefore every child, when it is brought to be baptized, promises, by its godfathers and godmothers, repentance and faith, when it comes to years of understanding. It is not God's slave, as the beasts are. It is God's child. But God does not wish it to remain merely His child, under tutors and governors, forced to do what is right outwardly, and whether it likes or not. God wishes each of us to become His son, His grown-up and reasonable son. To know who we are;—to work in His kingdom for Him;—to guide and manage our own wills, and hearts, and lives in obedience to Him;—to claim and take our share as men of God of the inheritance which He has given us. And that we can only do by faith in Jesus Christ. We must trust in Him, our Lord, our King, our Saviour, our Pattern. We must confess that we are nothing in ourselves, that we owe all to Him. We must follow in his footsteps, giving up our wills to God's will, doing not our own works, but the good works which God has prepared for us to walk in; and then we shall be truly confirmed; not mere children of God, under tutors, governors, schoolmasters and lawgivers, but free, reasonable, willing, hearty Christians, perfect men of God, the sons of God without rebuke.

Oh, my friends, will you claim your share in the Spirit of God, whom the Lord bought for us with His precious blood, that Spirit who was given you at your baptism, which may be daily renewed in you, if you pray for it; who will strengthen and lift you up to lead lives worthy of your high calling? Or will you, like Esau of old, despise your birthright, and neglect to pray that God's Spirit may be renewed in you, and so lose more and more day by day the thought that God is your Father, and the love of holy and godlike things? Alas! take care that, like Esau, you hereafter find no room for repentance, though you seek it carefully with tears! It is a fearful thing to despise the mercies of the living God; and when you are called to be His sons, to fall back under the terrors of His law, in slavish fears and a guilty conscience, and remorse which cannot repent.

And do not give way to false humility, says St. Paul. Do not say, 'This is too high an honour for us to claim.' Do not say, 'It seems too conceited and assuming for us miserable sinners to call ourselves sons of God. We shall please God better, and show ourselves more reverent to Him, by calling ourselves His slaves, and crouching and trembling before Him, as if we expected Him to strike us dead, and making all sorts of painful and tiresome religious observances, and vain repetitions of prayers, to win His favour;' or by saying, 'We dare not call ourselves God's children yet; we are not spiritual enough; but when we have gone through all the necessary changes of heart, and frames, and feeling, and have been convinced of sin, and converted, and received the earnest, God's Spirit, by which we cry, Abba, Father! then we shall have a right to call ourselves God's children.'

Not so, says St. Paul, all through this very Epistle to the Galatians. That is not being reverent to God. It is insulting Him. For it is despising the honour which He has given you, and trying to get another honour of your own invention, by observances, and frames, and feelings of your own. Do not say, 'When we have received the earnest of God's Spirit, by which we can cry, Abba, Father! then we shall become God's children;' for it is just because you are God's children already—just because you have been God's children all along, that God has taught you to call Him Father. The Lord Jesus Christ told men that God was their Father. Not merely to the Apostles, but to poor, ignorant, sinful wretches, publicans and harlots, He spoke of their Father in heaven, who, because He is a perfect Father, sends His sun to shine on the evil and the good, and His rain to fall on the just and on the unjust. The Lord Jesus Christ taught men—all men, not merely saints and Apostles, but all men, when they prayed—to begin, 'Our Father.' He told them that that was the manner in which they were to pray, and therefore no other way of praying can we expect God to hear. No slavish, terrified, superstitious coaxing and flattering will help you with God. He has told you to call Him your Father; and if you speak to Him in any other way, you insult Him, and trample under foot the riches of His grace.

This is the good news which the Bible preaches. This is the witness of God's Spirit, proclaiming that we are the sons of God; and, says St. Paul in another place, 'our spirit witnesses' to that glorious news as well. We feel, we know—why, we cannot tell, but we feel and know that we are the sons of God. When we are most calm, most humble, most free from ill-temper and self-conceit, most busy about our rightful work, then the feeling comes over us—I have a Father in heaven. And that feeling gives us a strength, a peace, a sure trust and hope, which no other thought can give. Yes, we are ready to say, I may be miserable and unfortunate, but the Great God of heaven and earth is my Father; and what can happen to me? I may be borne down with the remembrance of my great sins; I may find it almost too hard to fight against all my bad habits; but the Great God who made heaven and earth is my Father, and I am His son. He will forgive me for the past; He will help me to conquer for the future. If I do but remember that I am God's son, and claim my Father's promises, neither the world, nor the devil, nor my own sinful flesh, can ever prevail against me.

This thought, and the peace which it brings, St. Paul tells us is none of our own; we did not put it into our own hearts; from God it comes, that blessed thought, that He is our Father. We could never have found it out for ourselves. It is the Spirit of the Son of God, the Spirit of the Lord Jesus Christ, which gives us courage to say, 'Our Father which art in heaven,' which makes us feel that those words are true, and must be true, and are worth all other words in the world put together—that God is our Father, and we his sons. Oh, my friends, believe earnestly this blessed news! the news of Christmas-day, that you are not God's slaves, but his sons, heirs of God, and joint-heirs with Christ;—joint-heirs with Christ! In what? Who can tell? But what an inheritance of glory and bliss that must be, which the Lord Jesus Christ Himself is to inherit with us—an inheritance such as eye hath not seen, and incorruptible, undefiled, and that fadeth not away, preserved in heaven for us; an inheritance of all that is wise, loving, noble, holy, peaceful—all that can make us happy, all that can make us like God Himself. Oh, what can we expect, if we neglect so great salvation? What can we expect, if when the Great God of heaven and earth tells us that we are His children, we turn away and fall down, become like the brutes, and the savages, or worse, like the evil spirits who rebel against God, instead of growing up to become the sons of God, perfect even as our Father in heaven is perfect? May He keep us all from that great sin! May He awaken each and every one of you to know the glory and honour which Jesus Christ brought for you when He was born at Bethlehem—the glory and honour which was proclaimed to belong to you when you were christened at that font! May He awaken you to know that you are the sons of God, and to look up to Him with loving, trustful, obedient souls, saying from your hearts, morning and night 'Our Father which art in heaven,' and feeling that those words give you daily strength to conquer your sins, and feel assurance of hope that your Heavenly Father will help and prosper you, His family, every time you struggle to obey His commandments, and follow the example of His perfect and spotless Son, Jesus Christ the Lord!

DEATH IN LIFE

*Brethren, we are debtors, not to the flesh, to live after
the flesh. For if ye live after the flesh, ye shall die: but
if ye through the Spirit do mortify the deeds of the
body, ye shall live.*

Romans viii. 12, 13.

Does it seem strange to you that St. Paul should warn you, that
you are not debtors to your own flesh? It is not strange, when you
come to understand him; certainly not unnecessary: for as in his
time, so now, most people do live as if they were debtors to their
own flesh, as if their great duty, their one duty in life, was to please
their own bodies, and brains, and tempers, and fancies, and
feelings. Poor people have not much time to indulge their brains;
and no time at all, happily for them, to indulge their fancies and
feelings, as rich people do when they grow idle, and dainty, and
luxurious. But still, too many of them live as if they were debtors to
their own flesh; as if their own bodies and their own tempers were
the masters of them, and ought to be their masters. Young men, for
instance, how often they do things in secret of which it is a shame
even to speak, just because it is pleasant. Young women, how often
do they sell themselves and their own modesty, just for the pleasure
of being flattered and courted, and of getting a few fine clothes.
How often do men, just for the pleasure of drink, besot their souls
and bodies, madden their tempers, neglect their families, make
themselves every Saturday night, and often half the week, too, lower
than the beasts which perish. And then, when a clergyman
complains of them, they think him unreasonable; and by so
thinking, show that he is right, and St. Paul right: for if I say to you,
My dear young people (and I do say it), if you give way to filthy
living and filthy talking, and to drunkenness, and to vanity about
fine clothes, you will surely die—do you not say in your hearts, 'How
unreasonable: how hard on us! If we can enjoy ourselves a little,
why should we not? It is our right, and do it we will; and if it is
wrong, it ought not to be wrong.' Why, what is that but saying, that
you ought to do just what your body likes: that you are debtors to
your flesh; and that your flesh, and not God's law, is your master.

So again, when people grow older, perhaps they are more prudent about bad living, and more careful of their money: but still they live after the flesh. One man sets his heart on making money, and cares for nothing but that; breaks God's law for that, as if that was the thing to which he was a debtor, bound by some law which he could not avoid to scrape and scrape money together for ever. Another (and how often we see that) is a slave to his own pride and temper, which are just as much bred in his flesh: if he has been injured by any one, if he has taken a dislike against any one, he cannot forget and forgive: the man may be upright and kindly on many other points; prudent, too, and sober, and thoroughly master of himself on most matters; and yet you will find that when he gets on that one point, he is not master of himself; for his flesh is master of him: he may be a strong-minded, shrewd man upon most matters but just that one point: some old quarrel, or grudge, or suspicion, is, as we say, his weak point: and if you touch on that, the man's eye will kindle, and his face redden, and his lip tremble, and he will show that he is not master of himself: but that he is over-mastered by his fleshly passion, by the suspiciousness, or revengefulness, or touchiness, which every dumb animal has as well as he, which is not part of his man's nature, not part of God's image in him, but which is like the beasts which perish.

Now, my friends, suppose I said to you, 'If you give way to such tempers; if you give way to pride, suspicion, sullen spite, settled dislike of any human being, you will surely die;' should you not, some of you, be inclined to think me very unreasonable, and to say in your hearts, 'Have I not a right to be angry? Have I not a right to give a man as good as he brings?' so confessing that I am right, after all, and that some of you think that you are debtors to your flesh, and its tempers, and do not see that you are meant to be masters, and not slaves, of your tempers and feelings.

Again. Among poor women, as well as among rich ones, as they grow older, how much gossiping, tale-bearing, slandering, there is, and that too among people who call themselves religious. Yes, I say slandering; I put that in too; for I am certain that where the first two grow, the third is not far off. If gossiping is the root, tale-bearing and harsh judgment is the stem, and plain lying and slandering, and bearing false witness against one's neighbour, is the fruit.

Now I say, because St. Paul says it, 'that those who do such things shall surely die.' And do not some of you think me unreasonable in that, and say in your heart, 'What! are we to be tongue-tied? Shall we not speak our minds?' Be it so, my good women, only remember this: that as long as you say that, you confess that you are not masters of your tongues, but your tongues are masters of you, and that you freely confess you owe service to your tongue, and not to God. Do not therefore complain of me for saying the very same thing, namely, that you think you are debtors to your flesh—to the tongues in your mouths, and must needs do what those same little unruly members choose, of which St James has said, 'The tongue is a fire, a world of iniquity, and it sets on fire the whole course of nature, and is set on fire of hell.' And again: 'If any person among you seem to be religious, and bridles not his tongue, but deceives himself, that person's religion is vain.'

Again:—and, my good women, you must not think me hard on you, for you know in your hearts that I am not hard on you; but I must speak a word on a sin which I am afraid is growing in this parish, and in too many parishes in England; and that is deceiving kind and charitable persons, in order to get more help from them. God knows the temptation must be sore to poor people at times. And yet you will surely find in the long run, that 'honesty is the best policy.' Deceit is always a losing game. A lie is sure to be found out; as the Lord Jesus Himself says, 'There is nothing hid which shall not be made manifest;' and what we do in secret, is sure, unless we repent and amend it, to be proclaimed on the housetop: and many a poor soul, in her haste and greediness to get much, ends by getting nothing at all. And if it were not so;—if you were able to deceive any human being out of the riches of the world: yet know, that a man's life does not consist in the abundance of the things which he possesses. And know that if you will not believe that,—if you will fancy that your business is to get all you can for your mortal bodies, by fair means or foul,—if you will fancy that you are thus debtors to your own flesh, you will surely die: but if you, through the Spirit, do mortify the deeds of the body, you shall live.

And by this time some of you are asking, 'Live? Die? What does all this mean? When we die we shall die, good or bad; and in the meantime we shall live till we die. And you do not mean to tell us that we shall shorten our lives by our own tempers, or our tale-bearing, though we might, perhaps, by drunkenness?'

My friends, if such a question rises in your mind, be sure that it, too, is a hint that you think yourself a debtor to the flesh—to live according to the flesh. For tell me, tell yourselves fairly, is your flesh, your body, the part of yourself which you can see and handle, You?—You know that it is not. When a neighbour's body dies, you say, perhaps, 'He is dead,' but you say it carelessly; and when one whom you know well, and love, dies,—when a parent, a wife, a child, dies, you feel very differently about them, even if you do not speak differently. You feel and know that he, the person whom you loved and understood, and felt with, and felt for, here on earth, is not dead at all; you feel (and in proportion as the friend you have lost was loving, and good, and full of feeling for you, you feel it all the more strongly) that your friend, or your child, or the wife of your bosom, is alive still—where you know not, but you feel they are alive; that they are very near you;—that they are thinking of you, watching you, caring for you,—perhaps grieving over you when you go wrong—perhaps rejoicing over you when you go right,—perhaps helping you, though you cannot see them, in some wonderful way. You know that only their mortal flesh is dead. That their mortal flesh was all you put into the grave; but that they themselves, their souls and spirits, which were their very and real selves, are alive for evermore; and you trust and hope to meet them when you die;—ay, to meet them body and soul too, at the last day, the very same persons whom you knew here on earth, though the flesh which they wore here in this life has crumbled into dust years and ages before.

Is not this true? Is not this a blessed life-giving thought—I had almost said the most blessed and life-giving thought man can have— that those whom we have loved and lost are not dead, but only gone before; that they live still to God and with God; that only their flesh has perished, and they themselves are alive for evermore?

Now believe me, my friends, as surely as a man's flesh can die and be buried, while he himself, his soul, lives for ever, just so a man's self, his soul, can die, while his flesh lives on upon earth. You do not think so, but the Bible thinks so. The Bible talks of men being dead in trespasses and sins, while their flesh and body is alive and walking this earth. It talks, too, of a worse state, of men twice dead; of men, who, after God has brought their souls to life, let those souls of theirs die down again within them, and rot away, as far as we can see, hopelessly and for ever. And what is it which kills a man's soul within him on this side the grave, and makes him dead while he has a name to live? Sin, evil-doing, the disease of the soul, the death of the soul, yea, the death of the man himself. And what is sin but living according to the flesh, and not according to the spirit? What is sin but living as the dumb animals do, as if we were debtors to our own flesh, to fulfil its lusts, and to please our own appetites, fancies, and tempers, instead of remembering that we are debtors to God, who made us, and blesses us all day long;—debtors to our Lord Jesus Christ, who bought us with His own blood, that we might please Him and obey Him;—debtors to God's Holy Spirit, who puts into our minds good desires;—debtors to our baptism vows, in which we were consecrated to God, that He, and not this flesh of ours, might be our Master for ever?

This is sin; to give way to those selfish and evil tempers, against which I warned you in the beginning of my sermon, and which, if any man indulges in them, will surely and steadily, bit by bit, kill that man's soul within him, and leave the man dead in trespasses and sins, while his body walks this earth.

My friends, do not fancy these are merely farfetched words out of a book, made to sound difficult and terrible in order to frighten you. God forbid! When Scripture says this, it speaks a plain and simple truth, and one which I know to be a truth from experience. I speak that which I know, and testify that which I have seen. I have seen (and what sadder or more fearful sight?) dead men and dying walk this earth in flesh and blood; men busy enough, shrewd enough upon some points, priding themselves, perhaps, upon their cleverness and knowledge of the world, of whom all one could say was, The man is dead; the man is lost, unless God brings him to life again by His quickening Spirit: for goodness is dead in him; the powers of his soul are dead in him; the hope of being a better man is dead in him; all that God wishes to see him be and do, is dead; God's likeness and glory in him is dead: he thinks himself wise, and he is a fool in God's sight; for he sees not God's law, which is the only wisdom: he thinks himself strong, but he is utterly weak and helpless; for he is the slave of his own tempers, the slave of his own foul lust, the slave of his own pride and vanity, the slave of his own covetousness. Oh, my friends, people are apt to be afraid of what they call seeing a ghost—that is, a spirit without a body: they fancy that it would be a very shocking thing to meet one; but as for me, I know a far more dreadful sight; and that is, a careless and a hardened sinner—a body without a spirit. Which is uglier and ghastlier—a spirit without a body, or a body without a spirit? And yet such one meets, I dare not think how often.

What sadder sight, if you recollect that men need not be thus; that God hates seeing them thus; that they become thus, and die down in sin, in spite of God, with all heaven above, and God the Lord thereof, crying to them, Why wilt thou die? What sadder sight? How many have I seen, living, to all intents and purposes, as if they had no souls; as if there were no God, no Law of God, no Right, no Wrong; caring for nothing, perhaps, but drink and bad women; or caring for nothing but scraping together a little more money than their neighbours; or caring for nothing but dress, and vanity, and gossiping, and tale-bearing; and yet, when one came to know them, one saw that that was not what God intended them to be; that He had given them hearts which they had hardened, good feelings which they had crushed, sound brains which they had left idle, till one was ready to weep over them, as over something beautiful and noble ruined and lost; and looked on them as one would on a grand tree struck by lightning, decayed and dead, useless, and only fit to be burned, with just enough of its proper shape to show what a tree it ought to have been. And so it is with men and women: hardly a day passes but one sees some one of whom one says, with a sigh, 'What a worthy, loveable, useful person, that might have been! what a blessing to himself and all around him! and now, by following his fallen nature, and indulging it, he is neither worthy, nor loveable, nor useful; neither a blessing to himself nor to any human being: he might have been good for so much, and now he is good for nothing; for the spirit, the immortal soul which God gave him, is dead within him.'

My friends, I would not say this, unless I could say more. I would not say sad words, if I could not follow them up by joyful and hopeful ones. It is written, 'If ye live after the flesh, ye shall die;' but it is written also, 'If ye, through the Spirit, do mortify the deeds of the body, ye shall live.' It is promised—promised, my friends, 'Awake, thou that sleepest, and arise from the dead, and Christ shall give thee light.'

Through the Spirit, through God's Spirit, every soul here can live, now and for ever. Through God's Spirit, Christ not only can, but will, give you light. And that Spirit is near you, with you. Your baptism is the blessed sign, the everlasting pledge, that God's Spirit is with you. Oh, believe that, and take heart. I will not say, you do not know how much good there is in you; for in us dwells no good thing, and every good thought and feeling comes only from the Spirit of God: but I will say boldly to every one of you, you do not know how much good there may be in you, if you will listen to those good thoughts of God's Spirit; you do not know how wise, how right, how strong, how happy, how useful, you may become; you do not know what a blessing each of you may become to yourselves, and to all around you. Only make up your mind to live by God's law; only make up your mind, in all things, small and great, to go God's way, and not your own. Only make up your mind to listen, not to your own flesh, temper, and brain, which say this and that is pleasant, but to listen to God's Spirit, which says this is right, and that is wrong: this is your duty, do it. Search out your own besetting sins; and if you cannot find them out for yourself, ask God to show you them; ask Him to give you truth in the inward parts, and make you to understand wisdom in the secret places of your heart. Pray God's Spirit to quicken your soul, and bring it to life, that it may see and love what is good, and see and hate what is wrong; and instead of being most hard on your neighbour's sin, to which you are not tempted, be most hard on your own sin, on the sin to which you are most tempted, whatsoever that may be. You have your besetting sin, doubt it not; every one has. I know that I have. I know that I have inclinations, tempers, longings, to which if I gave way, my soul would rot and die within me, and make me a curse to myself, and you, and every one I came near; and all I can do is to pray God's Spirit to help me to fight those besetting sins of mine, and crush them, and stamp them down, whenever they rise and try to master me, and make me live after the flesh. It is a hard fight; and may God forgive me, for I fight it ill enough: but it is my only hope for my soul's life, my only hope of remaining a man worth being called a man, or doing my duty at all by myself and you, and all mankind. And it is your only hope, too. Pray for God's Spirit, God's strength, God's life, to give your souls life, day by day, that you may fight against your sins, whatsoever they are, lest they kill your souls, long before disease and old age kill your bodies. Make up your minds to it. Make up your minds to mortify the deeds of the body; to say to your own bodies, tempers, longings, fancies, 'I will not go your way: you shall go God's way. I am not your debtor; I owe you nothing; I am God's debtor, and owe Him everything, and I will pay Him honestly with the service of my body, soul, and spirit. I will do my duty, and you, my flesh, must and shall do it also, whether it is pleasant at first, or not:' and be sure it will be pleasant at last, if not at first. Keep God always before your eyes. Ask yourself in every action, 'What is right, what is my duty, what would God have me do?' And so far from finding it unpleasant, you will find that you are saving yourself a thousand troubles, and sorrows, and petty anxieties which now torment you; you will find that in God's presence is life, the only life worth having, and that at His right hand are pleasures for evermore. Oh, be sure, my friends, that in real happiness you will not lose, but gain without end. If to have a clear conscience, and a quiet mind; if to be free from anxiety and discontent, free from fear and shame; if to be loved, respected, looked up to, by all whose good word is worth having, and to know that God approves of you, that all day long God is with you, and you with God, that His loving and mighty arms are under you, that He has promised to keep you in all your ways, to prosper all you do, and reward you for ever,—if this be not happiness, my friends, what is?

SERMON XVIII

SHAME

*For the Scripture saith, Whosoever believeth on Him
shall not be ashamed.*

Romans x. 11.

My friends, what this text really means is one thing; what we
may choose to think it means is another thing—perhaps a very
different thing. I will try and show you what I believe it really
means.

'Whosoever believeth on Him shall not be ashamed.' It seems
as if St. Paul thought, that not being ashamed had to do with
salvation, and being saved; ay, that they were almost the same
thing: for he says just before, if thou doest so and so, thou shalt be
saved; for with the heart man believeth unto righteousness, and
with the mouth confession is made unto salvation; for the Scripture
saith, 'Whosoever believeth on Him shall not be ashamed;' as if
being ashamed was the very thing from which we were to be saved.
And certainly that wise and great man, whoever he was (some say
he was St. Ambrose, Bishop of Milan, in Italy), who wrote the Te
Deum, thought the same; for how does he end the Te Deum? 'O
Lord, in Thee have I trusted: let me never be confounded,' that is,
brought to shame. You see, after he has spoken of God, and the
everlasting glory of God, of Cherubim and Seraphim, that is, all the
powers of the earth and the powers of the heavens, of Apostles,
Prophets, Martyrs, the Holy Church, all praising God, and crying
'Holy, holy, holy. Lord God of Hosts, Heaven and Earth are full of
the majesty of Thy glory;' after he has spoken of the mystery of the
Trinity, Father and Son and Holy Ghost, of Christ's redemption and
incarnation, and ascension and glory; of His judging the world; of
His government, and His lifting up His people for ever; after he has
prayed God to keep them this day without sin, and to let His mercy
lighten upon them; after all this, at the end of this glorious hymn, all
that he has to say is, 'O Lord, in Thee have I trusted: let me never be
confounded.'—All he has to say: but that is a great deal: he does not
say that merely because he wants to say something more, and has
nothing else to say. Not so. In all great hymns and writings like
this, the end is almost sure to be the strongest part of all, to have the

very pith and marrow of the whole matter in it, as I believe this end of the Te Deum has; and I believe that whoever wrote it thought that being confounded, and brought to shame, was just the most horrible and wretched thing which could happen to him, or any man, and the thing above all others from which he was most bound to pray God to save him and every human being.

Now, how is this? First, let us look at what coming to shame is; and next, how believing in Christ will save us from it.

Now, every man and woman of us here, who has one spark of good feeling in them, will surely agree, that coming to shame is dreadful; and that there is no pain or torment on earth like the pain of being ashamed of oneself: nothing so painful. And I will prove it to you. You call a man a brave man, if he is afraid of nothing: but there is one thing the very bravest man is afraid of, and that is of disgrace, of coming to shame. Ay, my friends, so terrible is the torment of shame, that you may see brave men,—men who would face death in battle, men who would have a limb cut off without a groan, you may see such, in spite of all their courage, gnash their teeth, and writhe in agony, and weep bitter tears, simply because they are ashamed of themselves, so terrible and unbearable is the torment of shame. It may drive a man to do good or evil: it may drive him to do good; as when, rather than come to shame, and be disgraced, soldiers will face death in battle willingly and cheerfully, and do deeds of daring beyond belief: or it may drive him to do evil; rather than come to shame, men have killed themselves, choosing, unhappy and mistaken men, rather to face the torment of hell than the torment of disgrace. They are mistaken enough, God knows. But shame, like all powerful things, will work for harm as well as for good; and just as a wholesome and godly shame may be the beginning of a man's repentance and righteousness, so may an unwholesome and ungodly shame be the cause of his despair and ruin. But judge for yourselves; think over your past lives. Were you ever once—were it but for five minutes—utterly ashamed of yourself? If you were, did you ever feel any torment like that? In all other misery and torment one feels hope; one says, 'Still life is worth having, and when the sorrow wears away I shall be cheerful and enjoy myself again:' but when one has come to shame, when one is not only disgraced in the eyes of other people, but disgraced (which is a thousand times worse) in one's own eyes; when one feels that people have real reason to despise one, then one feels for the time as if life was not worth having; as if one did not care whether one died or not, or what became of one: and yet as if dying would do one no good, change of place would do one no good, time's running on would do one no good; as if what was done could not be undone, and the shame would be with one still, and torment one still, wherever one was, and if one was to live a million years: ay, that it would be everlasting: one feels, in a word, that real shame and deserved disgrace is verily and indeed an everlasting torment. And it is this, and the feeling of this, which explains why poor wretches will kill themselves, as Judas Iscariot did, and rush into hell itself, under the horror and pain of shame and disgrace. They feel a hell within them so hot, that they actually fancy that they can be no worse off beyond the grave than they are on this side of it. They are mistaken: but that is the reason; the misery of disgrace is so intolerable, that they are willing, like that wretched Judas, to try any mad and desperate chance to escape it.

So much for shame's being a dreadful and horrible thing. But again, it is a spiritual thing: it grows and works not in our fleshly bodies, but in our spirits, our consciences, our immortal souls. You may see this by thinking of people who are not afraid of shame. You do not respect them, or think them the better for that. Not at all. If a man is not afraid of shame; if a man, when he is found out, and exposed, and comes to shame, does not care for it, but 'brazens out his own shame,' as we say, we do not call him brave; we call him what he is, a base impudent person, lost to all good feeling. Why, what harder name can we call any man or woman, than to say that they are 'shameless,' dead to shame? We know that it is the very sign of their being dead in sin, the very sign of God's Spirit having left them; that till they are made to feel shame there is no hope of their mending or repenting, or of any good being put into them, or coming out of them. So that this feeling of shame is a spiritual feeling, which has to do with a man's immortal soul, with his conscience, and the voice of God in his heart.

Now, consider this: that there will surely come to you and me, and every living soul, a day of judgment; a day in which we shall be judged. Think honestly of those two words. First, a day, not a mere time, much less a night. Now, in a day there is light, by which men can see, and a sun in heaven which shows all things clearly. In that day, that brightest and clearest of all days, we shall see what we really have been, and what we really have done; and for aught we know, every one round us, every one with whom we have ever had to do, will see it also. The secrets of all our hearts will be disclosed; and we shall stand before heaven and earth simply for what we are, and neither more nor less. That is a fearful thought! Shall we come to shame in that day? And it will be a day of judgment: in it we shall be judged. I do not mean merely condemned, for we may be acquitted: or punished, for we may be rewarded; those things come after being judged. First, let us think of what being judged is. A judge's business is to decide on what we have done, or whether we have broken the law or not; to hear witnesses for us and against us, to sum up the evidence, and set forth the evidence for us and the evidence against us. And our judge will be the Son of Man, the Lord Jesus Christ, who is sharper than a two-edged sword, piercing through the very joints and marrow, and discerning the secret intents of the heart; neither is anything hid from Him, for all things are naked and open in the sight of Him with whom we have to do. With whom we have to do, mind: not merely with whom we shall have to do; for He sees all now, He knows all now. Ever since we were born, there has not been a thought in our heart but He has known it altogether. And He is utterly just—no respecter of persons; like His own wisdom, without partiality and without hypocrisy. O Lord! who shall stand in that day? O Lord! if thou be extreme to mark what is done amiss, who shall abide it? O Lord! in thee have I trusted: let me never be confounded!

For this is being confounded; this is shame itself. This is the intolerable, horrible, hellish shame and torment, wherein is weeping and gnashing of teeth; this is the everlasting shame and contempt to which, as Daniel prophesied, too many should awake in that day—to be found guilty in that day before God and Christ, before our neighbours and our relations, and worst of all, before ourselves. Worst of all, I say, before ourselves. It would be dreadful enough to have all the bad things we ever did or thought told openly against us to all our neighbours and friends, and to see them turn away from us;—dreadful to find out at last (what we forget all day long) that God knows them already; but more dreadful to know them all ourselves, and see our sins in all their shamefulness, in the light of God, as God Himself sees them;—more dreadful still to see the loving God and the loving Christ turn away from us;—but most dreadful of all to turn away from ourselves; to be utterly discontented with ourselves; ashamed of ourselves; to see that all our misery is our own fault, that we have been our own enemies; to despise ourselves, and hate ourselves for ever; to try for ever to get rid of ourselves, and escape from ourselves as from some ugly and foul place in which we were ashamed to be seen for a moment: and yet not to be able to get rid of ourselves. Yes, that will be the true misery of a lost soul, to be ashamed of itself, and hate itself. Who shall deliver a man from the body of that death?

I thank God, through Jesus Christ our Lord. I thank God, that at least now, here, in this life, we can be delivered. There is but one hope for us all; one way for us all, not to come to utter shame. And this is in the Lord Jesus Christ, who has said, 'Though your sins be red as scarlet they shall be white as wool; and their sins and their iniquities will I remember no more.' One hope, to cast ourselves utterly on His boundless love and mercy, and cry to Him, 'Blot these sins of mine out of Thy book, by Thy most precious blood, which is a full atonement for the sins of the whole world; and blot them out of my heart by Thy Holy Spirit, that I may hate them and renounce them, and flee from them, and give them up, and be Thy servant, and do Thy work, and have Thy righteousness, and do righteous things like Thee.' And then, my friends, how or why we cannot understand; but it is God's own promise, who cannot lie, that He will really and actually forgive these sins of ours, and blot them out as if we had never done them, and give us clean hearts and right spirits, to live new lives, right lives, lives like His own life; so that our past sinful lives shall be behind us like a dream, and we shall find them forgotten and forgiven in the day of judgment;—wonderful mercy! but listen to it—it is God's own promise—'If the wicked man turneth away from all his sins that he hath committed, and keep all my statutes, and do that which is lawful and right, he shall surely live, he shall not die. All his transgressions that he hath committed, they shall not be mentioned to him: in his righteousness that he hath done he shall live.'

They shall not be mentioned to him. My friends, if, as I have been showing, the great misery, the great horror of all, is having our sins mentioned to us in That Day, and being made utterly ashamed by them, what greater mercy can we want than this—not to have them mentioned to us, and not to come to shame; not to be plagued for ever with the hideous ghosts of our past bad thoughts, bad words, bad deeds, coming all day long to stare us in the face, and cry to us while the accusing Devil holds them up to us, as if in a looking-glass—'Look at your own picture. This is what you are. This fool, this idler, this mean, covetous, hard-hearted man, who cared only for himself;—this stupid man, who never cared to know his duty or do his duty;—this proud, passionate, revengeful man, who returned evil for evil, took his brothers by the throat, and exacted from them the uttermost farthing;—this ridiculous, foolish, useless, disagreeable, unlovely, unlovable person, who went through the world neither knowing what he ought to do, nor whither he was going, but was utterly blind and in a dream; this person is you yourself. Look at your own likeness, and be confounded, and utterly ashamed for ever!' What greater misery than that? What greater blessing than to escape that? What greater blessing than to be able to answer the accusing Devil, 'Not so, liar! This is not my likeness.

This ugly, ridiculous, hateful person is not I. I was such a one once, but I am not now. I am another man now; and God knows that I am, though you may try to shame me by telling me that I am the same man. I was wrong, but I am right now; I was as a sheep going astray, but now I am returned to the Shepherd and Overseer of my soul, to whom I belonged all the while; and now I am right, in the right road; for with the heart I have believed God unto righteousness, and He has given me a clean heart, and a right spirit, and has purged me, and will purge me, till I am clean, and washed me till I am whiter than snow; I do not deny one of my old sins; I did them, I know that; I confess them to thee now, oh accusing Devil; but I confessed them to God, ay, and to man too, long ago, and by confessing them to Him I was saved from them; for with the mouth confession is made unto salvation. And what is more; I have not only confessed my own sins, but I have confessed Christ's righteousness; and I confess it now. I confess, I say, that Christ is perfectly righteous and good, the Perfect Pattern of what I ought to be; and because He is perfectly good, He does not wish to see me remain bad and sinful, that He may taunt me and torment me with my sins, as thou the accusing Devil dost: but He wishes to make me and every man good like Himself, blest like Himself; and He can do it, and will do it, if we will but give up our hearts to Him; and I have given up my heart to Him. All I ask of Him is to be made good and kept good, set right and kept right; and I can trust in Him utterly to do that; for He is faithful and just to forgive me my sins, and cleanse me from all unrighteousness. Therefore, accuse me not, Devil! for thou hast no share in me: I belong to Christ, and not to thee. And set not my old sins before my face; for God has set them behind His back, because I have renounced them, and sworn an oath against them, and Christ has nailed them to His cross, and now they are none of mine and none of thine, but are cast long ago into the everlasting fire of God, and burnt up and done with for ever; and I am a new man, and God's man; and He has justified me, and will justify me, and make me just and right; and neither thou, nor any man, has a right to impute to me my past sins, for God does not impute them to me; and neither thou, nor any man, has a right to condemn me, for God has justified me. And if it please God to humble me more (for I know I want humbling every day), and to show me more how much I owe to Him—if it please Him, I say, to bring to light any of my past sins, I shall take it patiently as a wholesome chastening of my Heavenly Father's; and I trust to all God's people, and to angels, and the spirits of just men made perfect, that they will look on my past sins as God looks on them, mercifully and lovingly, as things past and dead, forgiven and blotted out of God's book, by the precious blood of Christ, and look on me as I am in Christ, not having any righteousness of my own, but Christ's righteousness, which comes by the inspiration of His own Holy Spirit.'

Thus, my friends, we may answer the Devil, when he stands up to accuse us, and confound us in the Day of Judgment. Thus we may answer him now, when, in melancholy moments, he sets our sins before our face, and begins taunting us, and crying, 'See what a wretch you are, what a hypocrite, too. What would all the world think of you, if they knew as much against you as I do? What would the world think of you, if they saw into that dirty heart of yours?' For we can answer him—'Whatever the world would think, I know what God Himself thinks: He thinks of me as of a son who, after wasting his substance, and feeding on husks with the swine, has come home to his Father's house, and cried, Father, I have sinned against heaven, and before Thee, and am no more worthy to be called Thy son; and I know that that same good Heavenly Father, instead of shaming me, reproaching me, shutting His doors against me, has seen me afar off, and taken me home again without one harsh word, and called to all the angels in heaven, saying, "It is meet that we rejoice and be glad, for this My son was dead and is alive again, he was lost and is found." And while Almighty God, who made heaven and earth, is saying that of me, it matters little what the lying Devil may say.'

Only, only, if you be wandering from your Father's house, come home; if you be wrong, entreat to be made right. If you are in your Father's house, stay there; if you are right, pray and struggle to keep right; if the old account is blotted out, then, for your soul's sake, run up no fresh account to stand against you after all in the Day of Judgment; if you have the hope in you of not coming to shame, you must purify yourselves, even as God is pure; if you believe really with your heart, you must believe unto righteousness; that is, you must trust God to make you righteous and good: there is no use trusting Him to make you anything else, for He will make you nothing else; being good Himself, He will only make you good: but as for trusting in Him to leave you bad, to leave you quiet in your sins, and then to save you after all, that is trusting that God will do a most unjust, and what is more, a most cruel thing to you; that is trusting God to do the Devil's work; that is a blasphemous false trust, which will be utterly confounded in the Day of Judgment, and will cover you with double shame. The whole question for each of us is, 'Do we believe unto righteousness?' Is righteousness what we want? Is to be made good men what we want? If not, no confessing with the mouth will be unto salvation, for how can a man be saved in his sins? If an animal is diseased can it be saved from dying without curing the disease? If a tree be decayed, can it be saved from dying without curing the decay? If a man be bad and sinful, can he be saved from eternal death without curing his badness and sinfulness? How can a man be saved from his sins but by becoming sinless? As well ask, Can a man be saved from his sins without being saved from his sins? But if you wish really to be saved from your sins, and taken out of them, and cured of them, that you may be made good men, righteous men, useful men, just men, loving men, Godlike men;—then trust in God for that, and you will find that your trust will be unto righteousness, for you will become righteous men; and confess God with your mouth for that, saying, 'I believe in God my Father; I believe in Jesus Christ His Son, who died, and rose, and ascended on high for me; I believe in God's Holy Spirit, which is with me, to make me right;' and your confession will be unto salvation, for you will be saved from your sins.

Always say to yourself this one thing, 'Good I will become, whatever it cost me; and in God's goodness I trust to make me good, for I am sure He wishes to see me good, more than I do myself; and you will find that because you have confessed, in that best and most honest of ways, that God is good, and have so given Him real glory, and real honour, and real praise, He will save you from the sins which torment you: and that because you have really trusted in Him, you shall never come, either in this world, or the world to come, to that worst misery, the being ashamed of yourself.

SERMON XIX

FORGIVENESS

Thou desirest not sacrifice; else would I give it: thou
delightest not in burnt offering.
The sacrifice of God is a broken spirit: a broken and a
contrite heart, O God, Thou wilt not despise.

Psalm li. 16, 17.

You all heard just now the story of Nathan and David, and you
must have all felt how beautiful, and noble, and just it was; how it
declares that there is but one everlasting God's law of justice, which
is above all men, even the greatest; and that what is right for the
poor man is right for the king upon his throne, for God is no
respecter of persons.

And you must have admired, too, the frankness, and fulness,
and humbleness of David's repentance, and liked and loved the man
still, in spite of his sins, as much almost as you did when you heard
of him as a shepherd boy slaying the giant, or a wanderer and an
outlaw among the hills and forests of Judæa.

But did it now seem strange to you that David's repentance,
which was so complete when it did come, should have come no
sooner? Did he need Nathan to tell him that he had done wrong?
He seduced another man's wife, and that man one of his most
faithful servants, one of the most brave and loyal generals of his
army; and then, over and above his adultery, he had plotted the
man's death, and had had him killed and put out of the way in as
base, and ungrateful, and treacherous a fashion as I ever heard of.
His whole conduct in the matter had been simply villanous. There
is no word too bad for it. And do you fancy that he had to wait the
greater part of a year before the thought came into his head that
that was not the fashion in which a man ought to behave, much
more a king?—that God's blessing was not on such doings as
those?—and after all not find out for himself that he was wrong, but
have to be told of it by Nathan?

Surely, if he had any common sense, any feeling of right and
wrong left in him, he must have known that he had done a bad
thing; and his guilty conscience must have tormented him many a

time and oft during those months, long before Nathan came to him. Now, that he had the feeling of right and wrong left in him, we cannot doubt; for when Nathan told him the parable of the rich man who spared all his own flocks and herds, and took the poor man's one ewe lamb, his heart told him that that was wrong and unjust, and he cried out, 'The man who has done this thing shall surely die.' And surely that feeling of right and wrong could not have been quite asleep in him all those months, and have been awakened then for the first time.

But more; if we look at two psalms which he wrote about that time, we shall find that his conscience had not been dead in him, but had been tormenting him bitterly; and that he had been trying to escape from it, and afterwards to repent—only in a wrong way.

If we look at the Thirty-second Psalm, we shall see there he had begun, by trying to deceive himself, to excuse himself before God. But that had only made him the more miserable. 'When I kept silence, my bones waxed old through my daily complaining. For Thy hand was heavy on me night and day: my moisture was turned to the drought of summer.' Then he had tried sacrifices. He had fancied, I suppose, that he could make God pleased with him again by showing great devoutness, by offering bullocks and goats without number, as sin-offerings and peace-offerings; but that made him no happier. At last he found out that God required no sacrifice but a broken heart. That was what God wanted—a broken and a contrite heart; for David to be utterly ashamed of himself, utterly broken down and silenced, so that he had nothing left to plead—neither past good deeds, nor present devoutness, nor sacrifices: nothing but, 'O God, I deserve all Thou canst lay on me, and more. Have mercy on me—mercy is all I ask.'

There was nothing for him, you see, but to make a clean breast of it; to face his sin, and all its shame and abomination, and confess it all, and throw himself on God's mercy. And when he did that, there, then, and at once, as Nathan told him, God put away his sin. As David says himself, 'I said, I will confess my sins unto the Lord, and so Thou forgavest the wickedness of my sin.'

As it is written, 'If we confess our sins, God is faithful and just to forgive us our sins, and to cleanse us from all unrighteousness.'

And now, my friends, what lesson may we learn from this? It is easy to say, We have not sinned as deeply as David, and therefore his story has nothing to do with us. My friends, whether we have sinned as deeply as David or not, his story has to do with you, and me, and every soul in this church, and every soul in the whole world, or it would not be in the Bible. For no prophecy of Scripture is of private interpretation; that is, it does not only point at one man here

and another there: but those who wrote it were moved by the Holy
Ghost, who lays down the eternal universal laws of holiness, of right
and good, which are right and good for you, and me, and all
mankind; and therefore David's story has to do with you and me
every time we do wrong, and know that we have done wrong.

Now, my friends, when you have done a wrong thing, you know
your conscience torments you with it; you are uneasy, and
discontented with yourselves, perhaps cross with those about you;
you hardly know why: or rather, though you do know why, you do
not like to tell yourself why.

The bad thing which you have done, or the bad tempers which
you have given way to, or the person whom you have quarrelled
with, hang in your mind, and darken all your thoughts: and you try
not to remember them: but conscience makes you remember them,
and will not let the dark thought fly away; till you can enjoy nothing,
because your heart is not clean and clear; there is something in the
background which makes you sad whenever you try to be happy.
Then a man tries first to deceive himself. He says to himself, 'No,
that sin is not what makes me unhappy—not that;' and he tries to
find out any and every reason for his uncomfortable feelings, except
the very thing which he knows all the while in the bottom of his
heart is the real reason. He says, 'Well, perhaps I am unhappy
because I have done something wrong: what wrong can I have
done?' And so he sets to work to find out every sin except the sin
which is the cause of all, because that one he does not like to face: it
is too real, and ugly, and humbling to his proud spirit; and perhaps
he is afraid of having to give it up. So I have known a man confess
himself a sinner, a miserable sinner, freely enough, and then break
out into a rage with you, if you dare to speak a word of the one sin
which you know that he has actually committed. 'No, sir,' he will
say, 'whatever I may be wrong in, I am right there. I have
committed sins too many, I know: but you cannot charge me with
that, at least;'—and all the more because he knows that everybody
round is charging him with it, and that the thing is as notorious as
the sun in heaven. But that makes him, in his pride, all the more
determined not to confess himself in the wrong on that one point;
and he will go and confess to God, and perhaps to man, all manner
of secret sins, nay, even invent sins for himself out of things which
are no sins, and confess himself humbly in the wrong where perhaps
he is all right, just to drug his conscience, and be able to say, 'I have
repented,'—repented, that is, of everything but what he and all the
world know that he ought to repent of.

But still his conscience is not easy: he has no peace of mind: he
is like David: 'While I held my peace, my bones waxed old through

my daily complaining.' God's hand is heavy on him day and night, and his moisture is like the drought in summer: his heart feels hard and dry; he cannot enjoy himself; he is moody; he lies awake and frets at night, and goes listlessly and heavily about his business in the morning; his heart is not right with God, and he knows it; God and he are not at peace, and he knows it.

Then he tries to repent: but it is a false, useless sort of repentance. He says to Himself, as David did, 'Well, then, I will make my peace with God: I will please Him. I have done one wrong thing. I will do two right ones to make up for it.' If he is a rich man, he perhaps tries David's plan of burnt-offerings and sacrifices. He says, 'I will give away a great deal in charity; I will build a church; I will take a great deal of trouble about societies, and speak at religious meetings, and show God how much I really do care for Him after all, and what great sacrifices I can make for Him.'

Or, if he is a poor man, he will say, 'Well, then, I will try and be more religious; I will think more about my soul, and come to church as often as I can, and say my prayers regularly, and read good books; and perhaps that will make my peace with God. At all events, God shall see that I am not as bad as I look; not altogether bad; that I do care for Him, and for doing right.'

But, rich or poor, the man finds out by bitter experience how truly David said, 'Thou requirest no sacrifice, else would I give it Thee. Thou delightest not in burnt-offerings.'

Not that they are not good and excellent; but that they are not good coming from him, because his heart is still unrepentant, because, instead of confessing his sin and throwing himself on God's mercy, he is trying to win God round to overlook his sin. So almsgiving, and ordinances, and prayer give the poor man no peace. He rises from his knees unrefreshed. He goes out of church with as heavy a heart as he went in, and he finds that for all his praying he does not become a better man, any more than a happier man. There is still that darkness over his soul, like a black cloud spread between him and God.

My friends, if any of you find yourselves in this sad case, the only remedy which I can give you, the only remedy which I ever found do me any good, or give me back my peace of mind, is David's remedy; the one which he found out at last, and which he spoke of in these blessed Psalms. Confess your sin to God. Bring it all out. Make a clean breast of it—whatever it may cost you, make a clean breast of it. Only be but honest with God, and all will come right at once. Say, not with your lips only, but from the very bottom of your heart, say, 'Oh, good God, Heavenly Father, I have nothing to say; I am wrong, and yet I do not know how wrong I am; but Thou knowest. Thou seest all my sin a thousand times more clearly than I do; and if I look black and foul to myself, oh God, how much more black and how foul must I look to Thee! I know not. All I know is, that I am utterly wrong, and Thou utterly right. I am shapen in sin, conceived in iniquity. My heart it is that is wrong. Not merely this or that wrong which I have done; but my heart, my temper, which will have its own way, which cares for itself, and not for Thee. I have nothing to plead; nothing to throw into the other scale. For if I have ever done right, it was Thou didst right in me, and not me myself, and only my sins are my own doing; so the good in me is all Thine, and the bad in me all my own, and in me dwells no good thing. And as for excusing myself by saying that I love Thee, I had better tell the truth, since Thou knowest it already—I do not love Thee. Oh God, I love myself, my pitiful, miserable self, well enough, and too well: but as for loving Thee—how many of my good deeds have been done for love of Thee? I have done right from fear of hell, from hope of heaven; or to win Thy blessings: but how often have I done right really and purely for Thy sake? I am ashamed to think! My only comfort, my only hope, is, that whether I love Thee or not, Thou lovest me, and hast sent Thy Son to seek and save me. Help me now. Save me now out of my sin, and darkness, and self-conceit. Show Thy love to me by setting this wrong heart of mine right. Give me a clean heart, oh God, and renew a right spirit within me. If I be wrong myself, how can I make myself right? No; Thou must do it. Thou must purge me, or I shall never be clean; Thou must make me to understand wisdom in the secret depth of my heart, or I shall never see my way. Thou must, for I cannot; and base and bad as I am, I can believe that Thou wilt condescend to help me and teach me, because I know Thy love in Jesus Christ my Lord. And then Thou wilt be pleased with my sacrifices and oblations, because they come from a right heart—a truly humble, honest, penitent heart, which is not trying to deceive God, or plaster over its own baseness and weakness, but confesses all, and yet trusts in God's boundless love. Then my alms will rise as a sweet savour before Thee, oh God; then sacraments will strengthen me, ordinances will teach me, good books will speak to my soul, and my prayers will be answered by peace of mind, and a clear conscience, and the sweet and strengthening sense that I am in my Heavenly Father's house, about my Heavenly Father's business, and that His smile is over me, and His blessing on me, as long as I remain loyal to Him and to His laws.' Feel thus, my friends, and speak to God thus, and see if the dark stupefying cloud does not pass away from your heart—see if there and then does not come sunshine and strength, and the sweet assurance that you are indeed forgiven.

But how about this old sin, which caused the man all this trouble? He began by trying to forget it. I think, if he be a true penitent, he will not wish to forget it any more. He will not torment himself about it, for he knows that God has forgiven him. But the more he feels God has forgiven him, the less likely he will be to forgive himself. The more sure he feels of God's love and mercy, the more utterly ashamed of himself he will be. And what is more, it is not wise to forget our own sins, when God has not forgotten them. For God does not forget our sins, though He forgives them; and a very bad thing it would be for us if He did, my friends. For the wages of sin is death: and even if God does not slay us for our sins, He is certain to punish us for them in some way, lest we should forget that sin is sin, and fancy that God's mercy is only careless indulgence. So God did to David. He then told him that though he was forgiven he would still be punished, 'The Lord has put away thy sin; nevertheless, the child that shall be born unto thee shall surely die.' Punishment and forgiveness went together. Ay, if we will look at it rightly, David's being punished was the very sign that God had forgiven him. Oh, believe that, my friends; face it; thank God for it. I at least do, when I look back upon my past life, and see that for every wrong I have ever done, I have been punished: not punished a tenth part as much as I deserve; but still punished, more or less, and made to smart for my own folly, and to learn, by hard unmistakable experience, that it will not pay me, or any man, to break the least of God's laws; and I thank God for it. I tell you to thank God also, whensoever you are punished for your sins. It is a sign that God cares for you, that God loves you, that God is training and educating you, that God is your Father, and He is dealing with you as with His sons. For what son is there whom His Father does not chastise? It is a bitter lesson, no doubt; but we have deserved it: then let us bear it like men. No doubt it is bitter: but there is a blessing in it. No chastisement at first seems pleasant, says the Apostle, but rather grievous: yet afterwards it yields the peaceable fruit of righteousness to those who are exercised thereby. Be exercised by it, then. Let God teach you in His own way, even if it seem a harsh and painful way. We have had earthly fathers, says the Apostle, who corrected us, and we gave them reverence. Shall we not much rather be in subjection to God, the Father of Spirits, and live? For suffering and punishment is the way to Eternal Life—to that true Eternal Life which is knowing God and God's love, and becoming like God. As the Apostle says, God chastens us only for our profit, that we may be partakers of His holiness. And as king Hezekiah says of affliction, 'Lord, by these things,' by sorrow and chastisement, 'men live; and in all these things is the life of the spirit.'

May God give to you, and me, and all mankind, as often as we do wrong, honest and good hearts to confess our sins thoroughly, and take our punishment meekly, and trust in God's boundless mercy, in order that if we humble ourselves under His rod, and learn His lessons faithfully in this life, we may not need a worse punishment in the life to come, but be accepted in the last great Day for the sake of Jesus Christ, our blessed Lord and Saviour.

SERMON XX

THE TRUE GENTLEMAN

*Covet earnestly the best gifts: and yet shew I unto you
a more excellent way. Though I speak with the
tongues of men and of angels, and have not charity, I
am become as sounding brass, or a tinkling cymbal.*

1 Cor. xii. 31; xiii. 1.

My friends, let me say a few plain words this morning to young and old, rich and poor, upon this text.

Now you all, I suppose, think it a good thing to be gentlemen and ladies. All of you, I say. There is not a poor man in this church, perhaps, who has not before now said in his heart, 'Ah, if I were but a gentleman!' or a poor woman who has not said in her heart, 'Ah, if I were but a lady!' You see round you in the world thousands plotting and labouring all their lives long to make money and grow rich, that they may become (as they think) gentlemen, or, at least, their sons after them. And those here who are what the world calls gentlemen and ladies, know very well that those names are names which are very precious to them; and would sooner give up house, land, money, all the comforts upon earth, than give up being called gentlemen and ladies; and these last know, I trust, what some poor people do not know, and what no man knows who fancies that he can make a gentleman of himself merely by gaining money, and setting up a fine house, and a good table, and horses and carriages, and indulging the lust of the flesh, and the lust of the eye, and the pride of life; for these last ought to know that the right to be called gentlemen and ladies is something which this world did not give, and cannot take away; so that if they were brought to utter poverty and rags, or forced to dig the ground for their own livelihood, they would be gentlemen and ladies still, if they ever had been really and truly such; and what is more, they would make every one who met them feel that they were gentlemen and ladies, in spite of all their poverty.

Now, people do not often understand clearly why this is. They feel, more or less, that so it is; but they cannot explain it. I could tell you why they cannot; but I will not take up your time. But if they cannot explain it, there are those who can. St. Paul explains it in the Epistle. The Lord Jesus Himself explains it in the Gospel. They tell us why money will not make a gentleman. They tell us why poverty will not unmake one: but they tell us more. They tell us the one only thing which makes a true gentleman. And they tell us more still. They tell us how every one of us, down to the poorest and most ignorant man and woman in this church, may become true gentlemen and ladies, in the sight of God and of all reasonable men; and that, not only in this life, but after death, for ever, and ever, and ever. And that is by charity, by love.

Now, if you will look two or three chapters back, in the Epistle to the Corinthians—at the 11th and 12th chapters—you will see that these Corinthians were behaving to each other very much as people are apt to do in England now. They all wanted to rise in life, and they wanted to rise upon each other's shoulders. Each man and woman wanted to set themselves up above their neighbours, and to look down upon them. The rich looked down on the poor, and kept apart from them at the Lord's Supper; and no doubt the poor envied the rich heartily enough in return. And these Corinthians were very religious, and some of them, too, very clever. So those who, being poor, could not set themselves up above their neighbours on the score of wealth, wanted to set themselves up on the score of their spiritual gifts. One looked down on his neighbours because he was a deeper scholar than they; another, because he had the gift of tongues, and understood more languages than they; another could prophesy better than any of them, and so, because he was a very eloquent preacher, he tried to get power over his neighbours, and abuse the talents which God had given him, to pamper his own pride and vanity, and love of managing and ordering people, and of being run after by silly women (as St. Paul calls them), ever learning and never coming to the knowledge of the truth. And of the rest, one party sided with one preacher, or one teacher, and another with another; and each party looked down on the other, and judged them harshly, and said bitter things of them, till, as St. Paul says, they were all split up by heresies, that is, by divisions, party spirit, envying, and grudging in the very Church of God, and at the very Table of The Lord.

Now says St. Paul, 'Covet earnestly the best gifts: and yet show I you a more excellent way;' and that is charity; love. As much as to say, I do not complain of any of you for trying to be the best that you can, for trying to be as wise as you can be, as eloquent as you can be, as learned as you can be: I do not complain of you for trying to rise; but I do complain of you for trying to rise upon each other's shoulders. I do complain of you for each trying to set up himself, and trying to make use of his neighbours instead of helping them; and, when God gives you gifts to do good to others with, trying to do good only to yourselves with them.

For he says, you are all members of one body; and all the talents, gifts, understanding, power, money, which God has bestowed on you, He has given you only that you may help your neighbours with them. Of course there is no harm in longing and praying for great gifts, longing and praying to be very wise, or very eloquent; but only that you may do all the more good. And, after all, says St. Paul, there is something more worth longing for, not merely than money, but more worth longing for than the wisdom of a prophet, or the tongue of an angel; and that is charity. If you have that, you will be able to do as much good as God requires of you in your station; and if you have not that, you will not do what God requires of you, even though you spoke with the tongues of men and of angels. Even though you had the gift of prophecy, and understood all mysteries, and all knowledge; even though you had all faith, so that you could remove mountains; even though you had all good works, and gave all your goods to feed the poor, and your body to be burned as a martyr for the sake of religion, and had not charity, you would be nothing. Nothing, says St. Paul, but sounding brass and a tinkling cymbal—an empty vessel, which makes the more noise the less there is in it. If you have charity, says St. Paul, you will be able to do your share of good where God has put you, though you may be poor, and ignorant, and stupid, and weak; but if you have not charity, all the wisdom and learning, righteousness and eloquence in the world, will only give you greater power of doing harm.

Yes, he says, I show you a more excellent way to be really great; a way by which the poorest may be as great as the richest,—the simple cottager's wife as great as the most accomplished lady; and that is charity, which comes from the Spirit of God. Pray for that— try after that; and if you want to know what sort of a spirit it is that you are to pray for and try after, I will tell you. Charity is the very opposite of the selfish, covetous, ambitious, proud, grudging spirit of this world. Charity suffers long, and is kind: charity does not envy: charity does not boast, is not puffed up: does not behave itself unseemly; that is, is never rude, or overbearing, or careless about hurting people's feelings by hard words or looks: seeketh not its own; that is, is not always looking on its own rights, and thinking about itself, and trying to help itself; is not easily provoked: thinketh no evil, that is, is not suspicious, ready to make out the worst case against every one; rejoiceth not in iniquity, but rejoiceth in the truth; that is, is not glad, as too many are, to see people do wrong, and to laugh and sneer over their failings: but rejoiceth in the truth, tries to find out the truth about every one, and judge them honestly, and make fair allowances for them: covereth all things; that is, tries to hide a neighbour's sins as far as is right, instead of gossiping over them, and blazoning them up and down, as too many do: believeth all things; that is, gives every one credit for meaning well as long as it can: hopeth all things; that is, never gives any one up as past mending: endureth all things, keeps its temper, and keeps its tongue; not rendering evil for evil, or railing for railing, but, on the contrary, blessing; and so overcomes evil with good.

In one word, while the spirit of the world thinks of itself, and helps itself, Charity, which is the Spirit of God, thinks of other people, and helps other people. And now:—to be always thinking of other people's feelings, and always caring for other people's comfort, what is that but the mark, and the only mark, of a true gentleman, and a true lady? There is none other, my friends, and there never will be. But the poorest man or woman can do that; the poorest man or woman can be courteous and tender, careful not to pain people, ready and willing to help every one to the best of their power; and therefore, the poorest man or woman can be a true gentleman or a true lady in the sight of God, by the inspiration of the Spirit of God, whose name is Charity.

They can be. And thanks be to the grace of God, they often are. I can say that I have seen among plain sailors and labouring men as perfect gentlemen (of God's sort) as man need see; but then they were always pious and God-fearing men; and so the Spirit of God had made up to them for any want of scholarship and rank. They were gentlemen, because God's Spirit had made them gentle. For recollect all, both rich and poor, what that word gentleman means. It is simply a man who is gentle; who, let him be as brave or as wise as he will, yet, as St. Paul says, 'suffers long and is kind; does not boast, does not behave himself unseemly; is not easily provoked, thinketh no evil.'

And recollect, too, what that word lady means. Most of you perhaps do not know. I will tell you. It means, in the ancient English tongue, a person who gives away bread; who deals out loaves to the poor. I have often thought that most beautiful, and full of meaning, a very message from God to all ladies, to tell them what they ought to be; and not to them only, but to the poorest woman in the parish; for who is too poor to help her neighbours?

You see there is a difference between a Christian man's duty in this and a Christian woman's duty, though they both spring from the same spirit. The man, unless he be a clergyman, has not so much time as a woman for actually helping his neighbours by acts of charity. He must till the ground, sail the seas, attend to his business, fight the Queen's enemies; and the way in which the Holy Spirit of Charity will show in him will be more in his temper and his language; by making him patient, cheerful, respectful, condescending, courteous, reasonable, with every one whom he has to do with: but the woman has time to show acts of charity which the man has not. She can teach in the schools, sit by the sick bed, work with her hands for the suffering and the helpless, even though she cannot with her head. Above all, she can give those kind looks and kind words which comfort the broken heart better than money and bodily comforts can do. And she does do it, thank God! I do not merely mean in such noble instances of divine charity and self-sacrifice as those ladies who have gone out to nurse the wounded soldiers in the East—true ladies, indeed, of whom I fear more than one, ere they return, will be added to the noble army of martyrs, to receive in return for the great love which they have shown on earth, the full enjoyment of God's love in heaven:—not these only, but poor women—women who could not write their own names—women who had hardly clothes wherewith to keep themselves warm—women who were toiling all day long to feed and clothe their own children, till one wondered when in the twenty-four hours they could find five spare minutes for helping their neighbours;—such poor women have I seen, who in the midst of their own daily work and daily care, had still a heart open to hear every one's troubles; a head always planning little comforts and pleasures for others; and hands always busy in doing good. Instead of being made hard and selfish by their own troubles, they had been taught by them, as the Lord Jesus was, to feel for the troubles of all around them, and went about like ministering angels in the Spirit of God, which is peace on earth and goodwill towards men.

Oh, my friends, such poor women seemed to me most glorious, most honourable, most venerable! What was all rank or fashion, beauty or accomplishments, when compared with the great honour which the Lord Jesus Christ was putting upon those poor women, by transforming them thus into His own most blessed likeness, and giving them grace to go about, as He the Lord Jesus did, doing good, because God was with them!

Then I felt that such women, poor, and worn, and hard-handed as they were, were ladies in the sight of that Heavenly Father, who is no respecter of persons; and felt how truly a wise ancient has said,—'It is virtue, yea, virtue, gentlemen, which maketh gentlemen; which maketh the poor rich, the strong weak, the simple wise, the base-born noble. This rank neither the whirling wheel of Fortune can destroy, nor the deceitful cavillings of worldlings separate; neither sickness abate, nor time abolish.' No; for it is written, that though prophecies shall fail, tongues cease, knowledge vanish away, and all that we now know is but in part, yet charity shall never fail those who are full of the Spirit of Love, but abide with them for ever and ever, bringing forth fruit through all eternity to everlasting life.

But what sort of virtue? Do not mistake that. Not what the world calls virtue; not mere legal respectability, which says, I do unto others as they do unto me; which is often merely the whitening outside the sepulchre, and leaves the heart within unrenewed, unrighteous, full of pride and ambition, conceit, cunning, and envy, and unbelief in God: not that virtue, but the virtue which the Apostle tells us to add to our faith, the virtue from above, which is the same as the wisdom from above, which is first pure, then peaceable, gentle, easy to be entreated; in one word, the Holy Spirit of God, the Spirit of Divine Love and Charity, which seeketh not its own, which St. Paul has described to us in this epistle; the Holy Spirit of God, with which the Lord Jesus was filled without measure, and which He manifested to all the world in His most blessed life and death.

Ah, my friends, this is not an easy lesson to learn. Christ's disciples and apostles could not learn it all at once. They tried to hinder little children from coming to Him. They rebuked the blind man who called after Him. How could the great Prophet of Nazareth stoop to trouble Himself about such poor insignificant people? They could not conceive, either, why the Lord Jesus should choose to die shamefully, when He might have lived in honour: it seemed unworthy of Him. They were shocked at His words. 'That be far from Thee, Lord,' said Peter. Afterwards, when they really understood what that word 'Lord,' meant, and what sort of a man a true and perfect Lord ought to be, then they saw how fit, and proper, and glorious, Christ's self-sacrifice was. When, too, they learnt to look on Him, not merely as a great prophet, but as the Son of the Living God, then they understood His conduct, and saw that it behoved an only-begotten Son of God to suffer all these things before He entered into His glory.

But the Scribes and Pharisees never understood it. To the last they were puzzled and angered by that very self-sacrifice of His: He must be a bad man, they thought, or He would not care so much for bad men. 'A friend of publicans and sinners,' they called Him, thinking that a shameful blame to Him, while it was really the very highest praise. But if they could not see the beauty of His conduct, can we? It is very difficult, I do not deny it, my friends, for the selfishness and pride of fallen man: it is difficult to see that the Cross was the most glorious throne that was even set up on earth, and that the crown of thorns was worth all the crowns of czars and emperors: difficult, indeed, not to stumble at the stumbling-block of the Cross, and to say, 'It cannot surely be more blessed to give than to receive:' difficult, not to say in our hearts, 'The way to be great is surely to rise above other men, not to stoop below them; to make use of them, and not to make ourselves slaves to them.' And yet the Lord Jesus Christ did so; He took on Himself the form of a slave, and made Himself of no reputation: and what was fit and good for Him, must surely be fit and good for us. But it is a hard lesson to the pride of fallen creatures: very hard. And nothing, I believe, but sorrow will teach it us: sorrow is teaching it some of us now. We surely are beginning to see, that to suffer patiently for conscience sake, is the most beautiful thing on earth or in heaven: we begin to see that those poor soldiers, dying by inches of cold and weariness, without a murmur, because it was their Duty, were doing a nobler work even than they did when they fought at Alma and Inkermann; and that those ladies who are drudging in the hospitals, far away from home, amid filth and pestilence, are doing, if possible, a nobler work still, a nobler work than if they were queens or empresses, because they have taken up the Cross and followed Christ; because they are not seeking their own good, but the good of others. And if we will not learn it from those glorious examples, God will force us to learn it, I trust, every one of us, by sorrow and disappointment. Ah, my friends, might one not learn it at once, if one would but open one's eyes and look at things as they are? Every one is longing for something; each has his little plan for himself, of what he would like to be, and like to do, and says to himself all day long, 'If I could but get that one thing, I should be happy: If I could but get that, then I should want no more!' Foolish man, self-deceived by his own lusts! Perhaps he cannot get what he wants, and therefore he cannot enjoy what he has, and is moody, discontented, peevish, a torment to himself, and perhaps a torment to his family. Or perhaps he does get what he wants: and is he happy after all? Not he. He is like the greedy Israelites of old, when they longed for the quails; and God sent the quails: but while the meat was yet in their mouths, they loathed it. So it is with a man's fancy. He gets what he fancies; and he plays with it for a day, as a child with a new toy, and most probably spoils it, and next day throws it away to run after some new pleasure, which will cheat him in just the same way as the last did; and so happiness flits away ahead before him; and he is like the simple boy in the parable, who was to find a crock of gold where the rainbow touched the ground: but as he moved on, the rainbow moved on too, and kept always a field off from him. You may smile: but just as foolish is every soul of us, who fancies that he will become happy by making himself great; admired, rich, comfortable, in short, by making himself anything whatsoever, or getting anything whatsoever for himself. Just as foolish is every poor soul, and just as unhappy, as long as he will go on thinking about himself, instead of copying the Lord Jesus Christ, and thinking about others; as long as he will keep to the pattern of the old selfish Adam, which is corrupt according to the deceitful lusts, the longings and fancies which deceive a man into expecting to be happy when he will not be happy; instead of putting on the new man, which after God's likeness is created in righteousness and true holiness: and what is true holiness but that very charity of which St. Paul has been preaching to us, the spirit of love, and mercy, and gentleness, and condescension, and patience, and active benevolence?

Ah, my friends, do not forget what I said just now; that a man could not become happy by making himself anything. No. Not by making himself anything: but he may by letting God make him something. If he will let God make him a new creature in Jesus Christ, then he will be more than happy—he will be blessed: then he will be a blessing to himself, and a blessing to every one whom he meets: then all vain longing, and selfishness, and pride, and ambition, and covetousness, and peevishness and disappointment, will vanish out of his heart, and he will work manfully and contentedly where God has placed him—cheerful and open-hearted, civil and patient, always thinking about others, and not about himself; trying to be about his Master's business, which is doing good; and always finding too, that his Master Christ sets him some good work to do day by day, and gives him strength to do it. And how can a man get that blessed and noble state of mind? By prayer and practice. You must ask for strength from God: but then you must believe that He answers your prayer, and gives you that strength; and therefore you must try and use it. There is no more use in praying without practising than there is in practising without praying. You cannot learn to walk without walking: no more can you learn to do good without trying to do good.

Ask, then, of God, grace and help to do good: Pray to Him this very day to take all selfishness and meanness out of your hearts, and to give you instead His Holy Spirit of Love and Charity, which alone can make you noble in His sight; and try this day, try every day of your lives, to do some good to those around you. Oh make a rule, and pray to God to help you to keep it, never, if possible, to lie down at night without being able to say, 'I have made one human being at least a little wiser, or a little happier, or a little better this day.' You will find it easier than you think, and pleasanter: easier, because if you wish to do God's work, God will surely find you work to do; and pleasanter, because in return for the little trouble it may cost you, or the little choking of foolish vulgar pride it may cost you, you will have a peace of mind, a quiet of temper, a cheerfulness and hopefulness about yourself and all around you, such as you never felt before; and over and above that, if you look for a reward in the life to come, recollect this—what we have to hope for in the life to come is, to enter into the joy of our Lord. And how did He fulfil that joy, but by humbling Himself, and taking the form of a slave, and coming not to be ministered to but to minister, and to give His whole life, even to the death upon the cross, a ransom for many? Be sure, that unless you take up His cross, you will not share His crown. Be sure, that unless you follow in His footsteps, you will never reach the place where He is. If you wish to enter into the joy of your Lord, be sure that His joy is now, as it was in Judæa of old, over every sinner that repenteth, every mourner that is comforted, every hungry mouth that is fed, every poor soul, sick or in prison, who is visited.

That is the joy of your Lord—to show mercy; and that must be your joy too, if you wish to enter into His joy. Surely that is plain. You must rejoice in doing the same work that He rejoices in, and then His joy and yours will be the same; then you will enter into His joy, and He will enter into yours; then, as St. John says, you will dwell in Christ, and Christ in you, because you love the brethren; and you will hear through all eternity the blessed words, 'Inasmuch as ye did it unto one of the least of these little ones, ye did it unto Me.'

SERMON XXI

TOLERATION

[Preached at Bideford, 1854]

> *And if in any thing ye shall be otherwise minded, God
> shall reveal even this to you. Nevertheless, whereto
> we have already attained, let us walk by the same
> rule, let us mind the same thing.*
>
> Philippians iii. 15, 16.

My friends, allow me to speak a few plain and honest words, ere
we part, on a matter which is near to, and probably important to,
many of us here. We all know how the Christian Church has in all
ages been torn in pieces by religious quarrels; we all know too well
how painfully these religious quarrels have been brought home to
our very doors and hearts of late.

Now, we all deplore, or profess to deplore, these differences and
controversies. But we may do that in two ways: we may say, 'I am
very sorry that all Christians do not think alike,' when all we mean
is, 'I am very sorry that all Christians do not think just as I do, for I
am right and infallible, whosoever else is wrong.' The fallen heart of
man is too apt to say that, my friends, in its pride and narrowness,
and while it cries out against the Pope of Rome, sets itself up as
Pope in his stead.

But there is surely another and a better way of deploring these
differences: and that is, to say to oneself, 'I am sorry, bitterly sorry,
that Christians cannot differ without quarrelling and hating one
another over and above.' And then comes the deeper home-
thought, 'And how much more sorry I am that I myself cannot differ
from my fellow-Christians without growing angry with them,
suspecting them, despising them, treating them as if they were not
my fellow-Christians at all.' Yes, my friends, this is what we have to
do first when we think of religious controversies, to examine our
own hearts and deeds and words; to see whether we too have not
been making bitterness more bitter, and, as the old proverb says,
'stirring the fire with a sword;' and to repent humbly and utterly of
every harsh word, hasty judgment, ungenerous suspicion, as sins,

not only against men, but against God the Father of Lights, who worketh in each of His children to will and to do of His good pleasure.

But some will say, 'We cannot give up what we believe to be right and true.' God forbid that you should try to do so, my friends; for if you really believe it, you cannot, even if you try; and by trying you will only make yourselves dishonest. But does not that hold as good of the man who differs from you? God will not surely lay down one law for you, and another for him? 'But we are right, and he is wrong.' Be it so. You do not surely mean that you are quite right; perfect and infallible? You mean that you are right on the whole, and as far as you see. And how can you tell but that he is right on the whole, and as far as he sees? You will answer that both cannot be right; that yes and no cannot be both true; that a thing cannot be black and white also.

My friends, my friends—but where is the religious controversy, the two sides whereof are as clearly opposite to each other as yes and no, black and white? I know none now; I have hardly found one in the records of the Protestant Church since first Luther and our Reformers protested against Romish idolatry. On that last matter there should be no doubt, as long as the first two commandments stand in the Decalogue; but, with that exception, it would be difficult to find a dispute in which the truth lay altogether with one party. The truth rather lies, in general, not so much halfway between the two combatants, as in some third place, which neither of them sees; which perhaps God does not intend them to see in this life, while He leaves his servants each to work out some one side of Christian truth, dividing to every man severally as He will, according to the powers of each mind, and the needs of each situation.

True we have the infallible rule of Scripture: but are our own interpretations of it so sure to be infallible? Inspired, infinite, inexhaustible as it is, can we pretend to have fathomed all its abysses, to have comprehended all its boundless treasures? The pretence is folly. True, again, it contains all things necessary to salvation; and those so plainly set forth, that he who runs may read, and the wayfaring man, though poor, shall not err therein. And yet does it not contain things whereof even St. Paul himself said, that he only knew in part, and prophesied in part, and saw as through a glass darkly; and are we to suppose that they are among the truths necessary to salvation? Now are not the points about which there has been, and is still, most dispute, just of this very number? Do they belong to the simple fundamental truths of the Gospel? No. Are they such plain matters that the wayfaring man, though poor, can make up his mind on them for himself? No. Are they one of them laid down directly in Scripture, like the Ten Commandments, the Lord's Prayer, or the Creeds? No. They are every one, as it seems to me, whether they be right or wrong, abstruse deductions, delicate theories, built up on single and obscure texts. Surely, if they had been necessary for salvation, the Lord would have spoken on them in a tone and in words about which there should be no more mistake than about the thunders of Sinai, and the tables of stone fresh from the finger-mark of God. And He has spoken to us, my friends, on other matters, if not on these. His promises are clear enough, and short enough, though high as heaven and wide as the universe. There is one God, and one Mediator between God and man, the man Christ Jesus, the only-begotten Son of God; and whosoever believeth that Jesus is the Christ, is born of God; and if any man sin, we have an Advocate with the Father, Jesus Christ the righteous, and He is the propitiation for our sins. And again, 'If any man lack wisdom, let him ask of God, who giveth liberally, and upbraideth not, and he shall receive it.' 'For if ye, being evil, know how to give good gifts to your children, much more shall your Heavenly Father give His Holy Spirit to them who ask Him.'

These are God's promises—simple and clear enough: and what are God's demands? Are they numerous, intricate, burdensome, a yoke which neither we nor our fathers have been able to bear? God forbid again!—'He hath showed thee, oh man, what is good. And what doth the Lord require of thee, but to do justly and to love mercy, and to walk humbly with thy God?' And lest thou shouldest mistake in the least the meaning of these words, He hath showed thee all this, and more, by a living example fairer than all the sons of men, and through lips full of grace, in the blessed life and blessed death of His Son Jesus Christ, the brightness of His glory, and the express image of His person. To this, at least, we have already attained. Let us walk by this rule, let us all mind this same thing, and if in anything else we are differently minded, God in His own good time will reveal even that to us.

Is not this enough, my friends? Then why should we bite and tear each other about that which is over and above this? If any man believes this, and acts on it, let us hail him as a brother. After all, let our differences be what they will, have we not one Lord, one faith, one baptism, one God and Father of all, who is above all, and through all, and in us all? If this is not bond enough between man and man, what bond would we have? Oh, my friends, when we consider this our little life, how full of ignorance it is and darkness; within us, rebellion, inconstancy, confusion, daily sins and shortcomings; and without us, disappointment, fear of loneliness,

loss of friends, loss of all which makes life worth having,—who are
we that we should deny proudly one single tie which binds us to any
other human being? Who are we that we should refuse one hand
stretched out to grasp our own? Who are we that we should say,
'Stand back, for I am holier than thou?' Who are we that we should
judge another? to his own master let him stand or fall—'yea, and he
shall stand,' says the Apostle, 'for God is able to make him stand.'

Think of those last words, my friends, they are strong and
startling; but we must not shrink from them. They tell us that God
may be as near those whom we heap with hard names, as He is near
to us; that He may intend that they should triumph, not over us, but
with us over evil. And if God be with them, who dare be against
them? Shall we be more dainty than God? And therefore I have
never been able to hear, without a shudder, words which I have
heard, and from really Christian men too: 'I can wish well to a pious
man of a different denomination from mine; I can honour and
admire the fruits of God's Spirit in him; but I cannot co-operate
with him.' When I hear such language from really good men, I
confess I am puzzled. I have no doubt that their reasons seem to
them very sound; but what they are I cannot conceive. I cannot
conceive why I should not hold out the right hand of fellowship and
brotherhood to every man who fears God and works righteousness,
of whatsoever denomination he may be. We believe the Apostles'
Creed, surely? Then think of the meaning of that one word, The
Holy Spirit. To whom are we to attribute any man's good deeds,
except to the Holy Spirit? We dare not say that he does them by an
innate and natural virtue of his own, for that would be to fall at once
into the Pelagian heresy; neither dare we attribute his good deeds to
an evil spirit, and say, 'However good they may look, they must be
bad, for he belongs to a denomination who cannot have God's
Spirit.' We dare not; for that would be to approach fearfully near to
the unpardonable sin itself, the sin against the Holy Ghost, the
bigotry which says, 'He casteth out devils by the Prince of the
devils.' Surely if we be Christians, and Churchmen, we confess (for
the Bible and the Prayer-book declare) that every good deed of man
comes down from the One Fountain of Good, from God, the Father
of Lights, by the inspiration of His Holy Spirit.

Then think, my friends, think what words we have said. We
confess that the great, absolute, almighty, eternal God, in whose
hand suns and stars, ages and generations, hell and heaven, and all
which is and has been, and ever will be, are but as a grain of sand;
who has but to take away His breath, and the whole universe would
become nothing and nowhere; the utterly holy and righteous God,
who is of purer eyes than to behold iniquity, who charges His angels

with folly, and the heavens are not clean in His sight—we confess, I say, that this great God has condescended to visit that man's soul, and cherish it, and teach it, and shape it (be it ever so little) into His own likeness: and shall we dare to stand aloof from him from whom God does not stand aloof? Shall we refuse to walk with one who walks with God? Shall we refuse to work with one who is a fellow-worker with God, to love one whom God loves, to take by the hand one whose guest God has become? Shall we be more dainty than God? more fastidious than God? more righteous than God? more separate from sinners than God? Oh, my friends, let us pray that we may love God better, and know His likeness more clearly; that we may be more ready to recognise, and admire, and welcome every, even the smallest trace of that likeness in any human being, remembering that it is the likeness of Christ, who was not merely The Teacher of all in every nation who fear God and work righteousness, but the Saviour who ate and drank with publicans and sinners: and then we shall be more careful how we call unclean what God Himself has cleansed with His own presence, His own grace, His own quickening and renewing and sanctifying Spirit.

Be sure, be sure, my friends, that in proportion as we really love the Lord Jesus Christ, we shall love those who love Him, be it in never so clumsy or mistaken a fashion; and love those too whom He loved enough to die for them, and whom He loves now enough to teach and strengthen. We shall say to them, not 'Wherein do we differ?' but 'Wherein do we agree?' Not, 'Because I cannot worship with you, therefore I will not work with you;' but rather, 'I wish that I could worship with you; I will whenever and wherever I can, as far as you allow me, as far as the law allows me, as far as your worship is not in my eyes an actually sinful thing: but, be that as it may, we can at least do together something better even than worshipping, and that is, working. We can surely do good together. Together, let our denomination or party be what it may, we can feed the hungry, clothe the naked, reform the prisoner, humanize the degraded, save yearly the lives of thousands by labouring for the public health, and educate the minds and morals of the masses, though our religious differences (shame on us that it should be so!) force us to part when we begin to talk to them about the world to come.'

For are we not brothers after all? Has not God made us of one blood, English men, with English hearts? Has not Christ redeemed us with one and the same sacrifice? Has not the Holy Spirit given us one and the same desire of doing good? And shall we not use that spirit hand in hand? Look, look at the opportunities of doing good which are around you; look at God's field of good works, white already to the harvest; and the labourers are few. Shall these few, instead of going manfully to work, stand idly quarrelling about the shape of their instruments, and their favourite modes of using them? God forbid! True, there are errors against which we are bound to protest to the uttermost; but how few? The one real enemy we have all to fight is sin—evil-doing. If any man or doctrine makes men worse—makes men do worse deeds, protest then, if you will, and spare not, and shrink not: for sin must be of the Devil, whatever else is not. And therefore we are bound to protest against any doctrine which parts man from God, and, under whatsoever pretence of reverence or purity, draws again the veil between him and his Heavenly Father, and denies him free access to the Throne of Grace, and the feet of Jesus, that he may carry thither his own sins, his own doubts, his own sorrows, and speak (wondrous condescension of redeeming grace!) speak with God face to face, and yet live. For this we must protest; for this we must die, if needs be; for if we lose this, we lose all which our reforming forefathers won for us at the stake, ay, we lose our own souls; for we lose righteousness and strength, and the power to do the will of God.

For to shut a man out from free access to God and Christ is to make him certainly false, dishonest, cowardly, degraded, slavish, and sinful; as modern Popery has made, and always will make, those over whom it really gains power. This is the root of our hereditary protest against Popery; not merely because we do not agree with certain of its doctrines, but because we know from experience, that as now taught by the Jesuits, with whom it has identified itself, its general tendency is to make men bad men, ignorant, dishonest, rebellious; unworthy citizens of a free and loyal state.

And there are practices against which congregations have a right to protest, not only as Christians, but as free Englishmen. Congregations have a right to protest against any minister who introduces obsolete ceremonies which empty his church and drive away his people. Those ceremonies may be quite harmless in themselves, as I really believe most of them are; many of them may be beautiful, and, if properly understood, useful, as I think they are; but a thing may be good in itself, and yet become bad by being used at a wrong time, and in a way which produces harm. And it is shocking, to say the least, to see churches emptied and parishes thrown into war for the sake of such matters. The lightest word which can be used for such conduct is, pedantry; but I fear at times lest the Lord in heaven should be using a far more awful word, and when He sees weak brethren driven from the fold of the Church by the self-will and obstinacy of the very men who profess to desire to bring all into the Church, as the only place where salvation is to be found,—I fear, I say, when I see such deeds, lest the Lord should repeat against them His own awful words: 'If any man scandalize one of these little ones who believeth on Me, it were better for him that a millstone were hanged about his neck, and that he were drowned in the depths of the sea.' What sadder mistake? Those who have sworn to seek out Christ's lambs scattered up and down this wicked world, shall they be the very ones to frighten those lambs out of the fold, instead of alluring them back into it? Shall the shepherd play the part, not even of the hireling who flees and leaves the sheep to themselves, but of the very wolf who scatters the flock? God forbid! The Church, like the Sabbath, was made for man, my friends: not man for the Church; and the Son of Man, as He is Lord of the Sabbath, is Lord of the Church, and will have mercy in its dealings rather than sacrifice. The minister, my friends, was made for the people: and not the people for the minister. What else does the very name 'minister' mean? Not a lord who has dominion, but a servant, a servant to all, who must give up again and again his private notions of what he thinks best in itself for the sake of what will be best for his flock; who must be, like St. Paul, a Jew to the Jews; under the law to those who are still under the law; and yet again without law to those who are without law (though not without law to God, but under the law to Christ); weak with the weak; strong with the strong; that he may gain men of all sorts of opinions and characters by agreeing with them as far as he honestly can, and showing his sympathy with each as much as he can; and so become all things to all men, that he may by all means save some. Oh, my friends, who can read honestly that glorious First Epistle to the Corinthians and not see how a man may have the most intense earnestness, the strongest doctrinal certainty, and yet at the same time the greatest freedom, and charity, and liberality about minor matters of ceremonies and Church arrangements, and practical methods of usefulness; glad even that Christ be preached by his enemies, and out of spite to him, because any way Christ is preached?

But, my friends, if it is the right of free Englishmen to protest against such doings, how shall it be done? Surely in gentleness, calmness, reverence, as by men who know that they are standing on holy ground, and dealing with sacred things, before the Throne of God, and beneath the eye of Jesus Christ. Not surely, as it has been too often done, in bitterness, and wrath, and clamour, and evil-speaking, with really unjust suspicions, exaggerations, slanders, (and those, too, anonymous,) in the columns of the public prints. My friends, these are not God's weapons. Not such is Ithuriel's magic spear, the very touch of which unmasks falsehood. This is to try to cast out Satan by Satan, to make evil worse by fighting it with fresh evil. Oh, my friends, if there is one counsel which I would press on all here more earnestly than another, it is this—never, never, howsoever great may be the temptation, to indulge in anonymous attacks on any human being. No man has a right to do it who prays daily to his Father in heaven, Lead us not into temptation. For it is to lead oneself into temptation, and that too sore to resist; into the temptation to say something which one dare not say, and ought not to say, were one's name known; the temptation to forget not only the charity of Christians, but even the courtesies of civilized life; and to shoot, from behind the safe hedge of anonymousness, coward and envenomed shafts, of which we should be ashamed, did the world know that they were ours; of which we shall surely be ashamed in that great day, when the secrets of all hearts shall be disclosed. I speak strongly: but only because I know by bitter experience the terrible truth of my own words.

And consider, my friends, can any good result come from handling sacred matters with such harsh and fierce hands as they have been handled of late? For ourselves, such evil tempers only excite, irritate, blind us: they prevent our doing justice to the opposite side—(I speak of all parties)—they put us into an unwholesome state of suspicion, and tempt us to pass harsh judgments upon men as righteous, and perhaps far more righteous, than ourselves: they stir up our pride to special plead our case, to make the best of our own side, and the worst of our opponents': they defile our very prayers; till, when we ought to be praying God to bless all mankind, we catch ourselves unawares calling on Him to curse our enemies.

For those who are without—for the infidel, the profligate, the careless—oh, what a scandal to them! What an excuse for them to blaspheme the holy name whereby we are called, and ask, as of old, 'Is this then the Gospel of Peace? See how these Christians hate one another!'

While for the young, oh, my friends, what a scandal, again, to them! If you had seen (as I have) pious parents destroying in their own childrens' minds all faith, all reverence for holy things, by mixing themselves up in religious controversies, and indulging by their own firesides in fierce denunciations of men no worse than themselves;—if you will watch (as you may) young people taking refuge, some in utter frivolity, saying, 'What am I to believe? When religionists have settled what religion is, it will be time enough for me to think of it: meanwhile, let me eat and drink, for to-morrow I die;'—and others, the children of strong Protestant parents, taking refuge in the apostate Church of Rome, and saying, 'If Englishmen do not know what to believe, Rome does; if I cannot find certainty in Protestantism, I can in Popery;'—if you will consider honestly and earnestly these sad tragedies, you will look on it as a sacred duty to the children whom God has given you, to keep aloof as much as possible from all those points on which Christians differ, and make your children feel from their earliest years that there are points, and those the great, vital root points, on which all more or less agree, which many members of the Romish Church have held, and, I doubt not, now hold, as firmly as Protestants,—adoption by one common Father, justification by the blood of one common Saviour, sanctification by one common Holy Spirit.

And believe me, my friends, that just in proportion as you delight in, and live by, these great doctrines, all controversies will become less and less important in your eyes. The more you value the living body of Christianity, the less you will think of its temporary garments; the more you feel the power of God's Spirit, the less scrupulous will you be about the peculiar form in which He may manifest Himself. Personal trust in Christ Jesus, personal love to Christ Jesus, personal belief that He and He only, is governing this poor diseased and confused world; that He is really fighting against all evil in it; that He really rules all nations, and fashions the hearts of all of them, and understands all their works, and has appointed them their times and the bounds of their habitation, if haply they may feel after Him and find Him: personal and living belief that the just and loving Lord Christ reigneth, be the peoples never so unquiet;—this, this will keep your minds clear, and sober, and charitable, and will make you turn with disgust from platform squabbles and newspaper controversies, to do the duty which lies nearest you; to walk soberly and righteously with your God, and train up your children in His faith and fear, not merely to be scholars, not merely to be devotees, but to be Christian Englishmen; courteous and gentle, and yet manful and self-restraining; fearing God and regarding man; growing up healthy under that solemn sense of national duty which is the only safeguard of national freedom.

And, meanwhile, you will leave all who differ from you in the hands of a God who wills their salvation far more than you can do; who accepts, in every nation, those who fear Him and work righteousness; who is merciful in this—that He rewards every man according to his work; and who, if our brothers be otherwise minded from us, will reveal even that to them, if we be right: or, again, to us, if they be right. For we may have to learn from them, as well as they from us; and both have to learn much from God, in the day when all controversies and doubts shall vanish like a cloud; when we shall see no longer in part, and through a glass darkly, but face to face; while all things shall be bright in the sunshine of God's presence and of the countenance of His Son Jesus Christ our Lord.

SERMON XXII

PUBLIC SPIRIT

(Preached at Bideford, 1855)

> *That there should be no division in the body; but that the members should have the same care, one of another. And whether one member suffer, all suffer with it; or whether one member be honoured, all rejoice with it.*
>
> 1 Corinthians xii. 25, 26.

I have been asked to preach in behalf of the Provident Society of this town. I shall begin by asking you to think over with me a matter which may seem at first sight to have very little to do with you or with a provident society, but which, nevertheless, I believe has very much to do with both, and is full of wholesome spiritual instruction for us all.

Did it ever happen to any of you, to see a mob of several thousands put to instant flight by a mere handful of soldiers? And did you ever ask yourself how that apparent miracle could come to pass? The first answer which occurred to you, perhaps, was, that the soldiers were well armed, and the mob was not: but soon, I am sure, you felt that you were doing the soldiers an injustice; that they would have behaved just as bravely if every man in that mob had been as well armed as they, and have resisted till they were overpowered by mere numbers. You felt, I am sure, that there was something in the hearts and spirits of those soldiers which there was not in the hearts of the mob; that though the mob might be boiling over with the greediest passions, the fiercest fury, while the soldiers were calm, cheerful, and caring for nothing but doing their duty, yet that there was a thought within them which was stronger than all the rage and greediness of the thousands whom they faced; that, in short, the seeming miracle was a moral and a spiritual miracle.

What, then, is this wonder-working thought which makes the soldier strong?

Courage, you answer, and the sense of duty. True; but what has called out the sense of duty? What has inspired the courage? There was a time, perhaps, when each of those soldiers was no braver or more steady than the mob in front of them. Has it never happened to you to know some young country lad, both before and after he has become a soldier? Look at him in his native village (if you will let me draw for you the sketch of a history, which, alas! is the history of thousands), perhaps one of the worst and idlest lads in it—unwilling to work steadily, haunting the public-house and the worst of company; wandering out at night to poach and caring for nothing but satisfying his gross animal appetites; afraid to look you in the face, hardly able to give an intelligible, certainly not a civil answer; his countenance expressing only vacancy, sensuality, cunning, suspicion, utter want of self-respect.

It is a sad sight, but how common a sight, even in this favoured land!

At last he vanishes; he has been engaged in some drunken affray, or in some low intrigue, and has fled for fear of the law, and enlisted as a soldier.

A year or two passes, and you meet the same lad again—if indeed he is the same. For a strange change has come over him: he walks erect, he speaks clearly, he looks you boldly in the face, with eyes full of intelligence and self-respect; he is become civil and courteous now; he touches his cap to you 'like a soldier;' he can afford now to be respectful to others, because he respects himself, and expects you to respect him. You talk to him, and find that the change is not merely outward, but inward; not owing to mere mechanical drill but to something which has been going on in his heart; and ten to one, the first thing that he begins to talk to you about, with honest pride, is his regiment. His regiment. Yes, there is the secret which has worked these wonders; there is the talisman which has humanized and civilized and raised from the mire the once savage boor. He belongs to a regiment; in one word, he has become the member of a body.

The member of a body, in which if one member suffers, all suffer with it; if one member be honoured, all rejoice with it. A body, which has a life of its own, and a government of its own, a duty of its own, a history of its own, an allegiance to a sovereign, all which are now his life, his duty, his history, his allegiance; he does not now merely serve himself and his own selfish lusts: he serves the Queen. His nature is not changed, but the thought that he is the member of an honourable body has raised him above his nature. If he forgets that, and thinks only of himself, he will become selfish sluttish, drunken, cowardly, a bad soldier; as long as he remembers it, he is a hero. He can face mobs now, and worse than mobs: he can face hunger and thirst, fatigue, danger, death itself, because he is the member of a body. For those know little, little of human nature and its weakness, who fancy that mere brute courage, as of an angry lion, will ever avail, or availed a few short weeks ago, to spur our thousands up the steeps of Alma, or across the fatal plain of Balaklava, athwart the corpses of their comrades, upon the deadly throats of Russian guns. A nobler feeling, a more heavenly thought was needed (and when needed, thanks to God, it came!) to keep each raw lad, nursed in the lap of peace, true to his country and his Queen through the valley of the shadow of death. Not mere animal fierceness: but that tattered rag which floated above his head, inscribed with the glorious names of Egypt or Corunna, Toulouse or Waterloo, that it was which raised him into a hero: he had seen those victories; the men who conquered there were dead long since: but the regiment still lived, its history still lived, its honour lived, and that history, that honour were his, as well as those old dead warriors': he had fought side by side with them in spirit, though not in the flesh; and now his turn was come, and he must do as they did, and for their sakes, and count his own life a worthless thing for the sake of the body which he belonged to: he, but two years ago the idle, selfish country lad, now stumbling cheerful on in the teeth of the iron hail, across ground slippery with his comrades' blood, not knowing whether the next moment his own blood might not swell the ghastly stream. What matter? They might kill him, but they could not kill the regiment: it would live on and conquer; ay, and should conquer, if his life could help on its victory; and then its honour would be his, its reward be his, even when his corpse lay pierced with wounds, stiffening beneath a foreign sky.

Here, my friends, is one example of the blessed power of fellow feeling, public spirit, the sense of belonging to a body whose members have not merely a common interest, but a common duty, a common honour.

This Christian country, thank God! gives daily many another example of the same: and every place, and every station affords to each one of us opportunities,—more, alas, I fear, than we shall ever take full advantage of: but I have chosen the case of the soldier, not merely because it is perhaps the most striking and affecting, but because I wish to see, and trust in God that I shall see, those who remain at home in safety emulating the public spirit and self-sacrifice which our soldiers are showing abroad; and by sacrifices more peaceful and easy, but still well-pleasing unto God, showing that they too have been raised above selfishness, by the glorious thought that they are members of a body.

For, are we not members of a body, my friends? Are we not members of the Body of bodies, members of Christ, children of God,

inheritors of the Kingdom of Heaven? Members of Christ—we, and
the poor for whom I plead, as well as we; perhaps, considering their
many trials and our few trials, more faithfully and loyally by far than
we are. There are some here, I doubt not, to whom that word, that
argument, is enough: to whom it is enough to say, Remember that
the Lord whom you love loves that shivering, starving wretch as well
as He loves you, to open and exhaust at once their heart, their
purse, their labour of love. God's blessing be upon all such! But it
would be hypocrisy in me, my friends, to speak to this, or any
congregation, as if all were of that temper of mind. It is not one in
ten, alas! in the present divided state of religious parties, who feels
the mere name of Christ enough of a bond to make him sacrifice
himself for his fellow Christians, as a soldier does for his fellow
soldiers. Not one in ten, alas! feels that he owes the same allegiance
to Christ as the soldier does to his Queen; that the honour of
Christianity is his honour, the history of Christianity his history, the
life of Christianity his life. Would that it were so: but it is not so.
And I must appeal to feelings in you less wide, honourable and
righteous though they are: I must appeal to your public spirit as
townsmen of this place.

I have a right as a clergyman to do so: I have a duty as a
clergyman to do so. For your being townsmen of this place is not a
mere material accident depending on your living in one house
instead of another. It is a spiritual matter; it is a question of
eternity. Your souls and spirits influence each other; your tastes,
opinions, tempers, habits, make those of your neighbours better or
worse; you feel it in yourselves daily. Look at it as a proof that,
whether you will or not, you are one body, of which all the members
must more or less suffer and rejoice together; that you have a
common weal, a common interest; that God has knit you together;
that you cannot part yourselves even if you will; and that you can be
happy and prosperous only by acknowledging each other as
brothers, and by doing to each other as you would they should do
unto you.

It may be hard at times to bring this thought home to our
minds: but it is none the less true because we forget it; and if we do
not choose to bring it home to our own minds, it will be sooner or
later brought home to them whether we choose or not.

For bear in mind, that St. Paul does not say, if one member
suffers, all the rest ought to suffer with it: he says that they do suffer
with it. He does not say merely, that we ought to feel for our fellow
townsmen; he says, that God has so tempered the body together as
to force one member to have the same care of the others as of itself;
that if we do not care to feel for them, we shall be made to feel with

them. One limb cannot choose whether or not it will feel the disease of another limb. If one limb be in pain, the whole body must be uneasy, whether it will or not. And if one class in a town, or parish, or county, be degraded, or in want, the whole town, or parish, or county, must be the worse for it. St. Paul is not preaching up sentimental sympathy: he is telling you of a plain fact. He is not saying, 'It is a very fine and saintly thing, and will increase your chance of heaven, to help the poor.' He is saying, 'If you neglect the poor, you neglect yourself; if you degrade the poor, you degrade yourself. His poverty, his carelessness, his immorality, his dirt, his ill-health, will punish you; for you and he are members of the same body, knit together inextricably for weal or woe, by the eternal laws according to which the Lord Jesus Christ has constituted human society; and if you break those laws, they will avenge themselves.'— My friends, do we not see them avenge themselves daily? The slave-holder refuses to acknowledge that his slave is a member of the same body as himself; but he does not go unpunished: the degradation to which he has brought his slave degrades him, by throwing open to him. the downward path of lust, laziness, ungoverned and tyrannous tempers, and the other sins which have in all ages, slowly but surely, worked the just ruin of slave-holding states. The sinner is his own tempter, and the sinner is his own executioner: he lies in wait for his own life (says Solomon) when he lies in wait for his brother's. Do you see the same law working in our own free country? If you leave the poor careless and filthy, you can obtain no good servants: if you leave them profligate, they make your sons profligate also: if you leave them tempted by want, your property is unsafe: if you leave them uneducated, reckless, improvident, you cannot get your work properly done, and have to waste time and money in watching your workmen instead of trusting them. Why, what are all poor-rates and county-rates, if you will consider, but God's plain proof to us, that the poor are members of the same body as ourselves; and that if we will not help them of our own free will, we shall find it necessary to help them against our will: that if we will not pay a little to prevent them becoming pauperized or criminal, we must pay a great deal to keep them when they have become so? We may draw a lesson—and a most instructive one it is—from the city of Liverpool, in which it was lately proved that crime—and especially the crime of uneducated boys and girls—had cost, in the last few years, the city many times more than it would cost to educate, civilize, and depauperize the whole rising generation of that city, and had been a tax upon the capital and industry of Liverpool, so enormous that they would have submitted to it from no Government on earth; and yet they had been blindly inflicting it upon themselves for years, simply because they chose to forget that they were their brothers' keepers.

Look again at preventible epidemics, like cholera. All the great towns of England have discovered, what you I fear are discovering also, that the expense of a pestilence, and of the widows and orphans which it creates, is far greater than the expense of putting a town into such a state of cleanliness as would defy the entrance of the disease. So it is throughout the world. Nothing is more expensive than penuriousness; nothing more anxious than carelessness; and every duty which is bidden to wait, returns with seven fresh duties at its back.

Yes, my friends, we are members of a body; and we must realize that fact by painful experience, if we refuse to realize it in public spirit and brotherly kindness, and the approval of a good conscience, and the knowledge that we are living like our Lord and Master Jesus Christ, who laboured for all but Himself, cared for all but Himself; who counted not His own life dear to Himself that by laying it down He might redeem into His own likeness the beings whom He had made; and who has placed us on this earth, each in his own station, each in his own parish, that we might follow in His footsteps, and live by His Spirit, which is the spirit of love and fellow-feeling, that new and risen life of His, which is the life of duty, honour, and self-sacrifice.

Yes. Let us look rather at this brighter side of the question, my friends, than at the darker. I will preach the Gospel to you rather than the Law. I will appeal to your higher feelings rather than to your lower; to your love rather than your fear; to your honour rather than your self-interest. It will be pleasanter for me: it will meet with a more cordial response, I doubt not, from you.

Some dislike appeals to honour. I cannot, as long as St. Paul himself appeals to it so often, both in the individual and in bodies. His whole Epistle to Philemon is an appeal, most delicate and graceful, to Philemon's sense of honour—to the thought of what he owed Paul, of what Paul wished him to repay, not with money, but with generosity.

And his appeal to the Corinthians is a direct appeal to their honour: not to fears of any punishment, or wrath of God, but to the respect which they owed to themselves as members of a body, the Church of Corinth; and to the respect which they owed to that body as a whole, and which they had disgraced by allowing an open scandal in it.

And his appeal was successful: they took it just as it was meant; and he rejoices in the thought that they did so. 'For this, that ye sorrowed after a godly sort, what carefulness it wrought in you, yea, what clearing of yourselves, what indignation, what fear, what vehement desire, what zeal, what revenge! In all things you have approved yourselves to be clear in this matter,'

Noble words, and nobly answered. My friends, you, too, are members of a body: go, and do likewise in the matter of this Society's failing funds.

* * * * *

May I boldly ask you to alter this to-day? This, remember, is no common day. It is a day of thankfulness. The thankfulness which you professed, and I doubt not many of you felt, on Thursday night, has not evaporated, I trust, by Sunday morning. You have not yet forgotten—I trust that there is many a one who will never forget—what you owe as townsmen of this place, to God who has preserved you safe through the dangers and sorrows of the past autumn. You owe more than one debt to God. You owe, all England owes, thanks to Him for the late bounteous harvest, thanks to Him for the present prosperous seed-time: think what our state might have been with scarcity, as well as war, upon us, and pay part of your debt this day. You owe a thank-offering for the cessation of the cholera; a thank-offering for the sparing of your own lives;—pay it now. You owe a thank-offering for the glorious victories of our armies:—pay it now. You belong, too, to an honourable body, which has a noble history, and sets you many a noble example; show yourselves worthy of that body, that history, those examples, now.

And what fitter place than this very church to awaken within you the thought of duty and of public spirit?—this church which stands as God's own sign that you are the townsmen, the representatives, ay, some of you the very descendants, of many a noble spirit of old time?—this church, in which God's blessing has been invoked on deeds of patriotism and enterprise, of which the whole world now bears the fruit?—these walls, in which Elizabeth's heroes, your ancestors, have prayed before sailing against the Spanish Armada,—these walls, which saw the baptism of the first red Indian convert, and the gathering in, as it were, of the firstfruits of the heathen,—these walls, in which the early settlers of Virginia have invoked God's blessing on those tiny ventures which were destined to become the seeds of a mighty nation, and the starting-point of the United States,—these walls, which still bear the monument of your heroic townsman Strange, who expended for his plague-stricken brethren, talents, time, wealth, and at last life itself. For, to return, and to apply, I hope, to your consciences, the example of the soldier with which I began this Sermon:—shall it be only on the battle-field that the power of fellow-feeling is shown forth? Shall public spirit be only strong when it has to destroy, and not when it has to save and comfort? God forbid! Surely you here have a common corporate life, common history, common allegiance, common interest, which should inspire you to do your duty, whatsoever it may be, for the good of your native place, and to show that you feel an honourable self-respect in the thought that you belong to an ancient and once famous town, which though it may be outstripped awhile in the race of commerce, need never be outstripped, if you will be worthy sons of your worthy ancestors, in that race to which St. Paul exhorts us; the race of justice and benevolence, the noble rivalry of noble deeds.

Oh, look, I beseech you, upon this church as its old worshippers, the forefathers of many of you who sit here this day, were wont to look on it. Remember that this church is the sign that you are one town, one parish, one body; that century after century, this church has stood to witness to your fathers, and your fathers' fathers, that all who kneel within these walls are brothers, rich or poor; that all are children of one Father, redeemed by one Saviour, taught by one Spirit. This, this is the blessed truth of which the parish church is token, as nought else can be—that you are one body, members one of another, and that God's blessing is on your union and fellow-feeling; that God smiles on your bearing each other's burdens, and so fulfilling the law of Christ. Look on this church, and do to others as this church witnesses that God has done for you.

And now, some of you may perhaps have been disappointed, some a little scornful, at my having used so many words about so small a matter, and talked of battles, legends, heroes of old time, all merely to induct you to help this Society with a paltry extra thirty pounds. Be it so. I shall be glad if you think so. If the matter be so small, it is the more easily done; if the sum be paltry, it is the more easily found. If my reasons are very huge and loud-sounding, and the result at which I aim very light, the result ought to follow all the more certainly; for believe me, my friends, the reasons are good ones, Scriptural ones, practical ones, and ought to produce the result. I give you the strongest arguments for showing your Christian, English public spirit; and then I ask you to show it in a very small matter. But be sure that to do what I ask of you to do to-day is just as much your duty, small as it may seem, as it would be, were you soldiers, to venture your lives in the cause of your native land. Duty, be it in a small matter or a great, is duty still; the command of Heaven, the eldest voice of God. And, believe me, my friends, that it is only they who are faithful in a few things who will be faithful over many things; only they who do their duty in everyday and trivial matters who will fulfil them on great occasions. We all honour and admire the heroes of Alma and Balaklava; we all trust in God that we should have done our duty also in their place. The best test of that, my friends, is, can we do our duty in our own place? Here the duty is undeniable, plain, easy. Here is a Society instituted for one purpose, which has, in order to exist, to appropriate the funds destined for quite a different purpose. Both purposes are excellent; but they are different. The Offertory money is meant for the sick, the widow, and the orphan; for those who cannot help themselves. The Provident Society is meant to encourage those who can help themselves to do so. Every farthing, therefore, taken from the Offertory money is taken from the widow and the orphan. I ask you whether this is right and just? I appeal, not merely to your prudence and good sense, in asking you to promote prudence and good sense among the poor by the Provident Society; I appeal to your honour and compassion, on behalf of the sick, the widow, and orphan, that they may have the full enjoyment of the funds intended for them. Again, I say, this may seem a small matter to you, and I may seem to be using too many words about it. Small? Nothing is small which affects not merely the temporal happiness, but the eternal welfare, of an immortal soul. My friends, my friends, if any one of you had to support yourself and your children on four, seven, or even (mighty sum!) ten shillings a week, it would not seem a small matter to you then. A few shillings more or less would be to you then a treasure won or lost; a matter to you of whether you should keep a house over your children's heads, whether you should keep shoes upon their feet, and clothes upon their backs; whether you should see them, as they grew up, tempted by want into theft or profligacy; whether you should rise in the morning free enough from the sickening load of anxiety, and the care which eats out the core of life, and makes men deaf and blind (as it does many a one) to all pleasant sights, and sounds, and thoughts, till the very sunlight seems blotted out of heaven by that black cloud of care—care—care—which rises with you in the morning, and dogs you at your work all day (even if you are happy enough to have work), and sits on your pillow all night long, ready to whisper in your ear each time you wake; 'Be anxious and troubled about many things! What wilt thou eat, and what wilt thou drink, and wherewithal wilt thou be clothed? For thou hast no Heavenly Father, none above who knowest that thou needest these things before thou askest Him.' Oh, my friends, if you had felt but for a single day, that terrible temptation, the temptation of poverty, and debt, and care, which leads so many a one to sell their souls for a few paltry pence, to them of as much value as pounds would be to you;—if, I say, you had once felt that temptation in all its weight, you would not merely sacrifice, as I ask you now to do, some superfluity, which you will never miss; you would, I do believe, if you had human hearts within you, be ready to sacrifice even the comforts of life to prevent him whose heart may be breaking slowly, not a hundred yards from your own door, (and more hearts break in this world than you fancy, my friends,) from passing through that same dark shadow of want, and care, and temptation where the Devil stands calling to the poor man all day long, 'Fall down, and worship me; and I will relieve those wants of thine which man neglects!'

I have no more to say. I leave the rest to your own good feeling, as townsmen of this ancient and honourable place,—remembering always who it was who said, 'Inasmuch as ye have done it unto one of the least of these my brethren, ye have done it unto Me.'

THE END